O9-BUD-214

Basic Black

The Essential Guide

for Getting Ahead at

Work (and in Life)

CROWN
BUSINESS
NEW YORK

Basic Black

Cathie Black

Crown Business is a trademark and the Rising Sun colophon
is a registered trademark of Random House, Inc.

Library of Congress Cataloging-in-Publication Data
Black, Cathie.
Basic Black : the essential guide for getting ahead at work
(and in life) / Cathie Black. — 1st ed.
p. cm.
1. Career development. 2. Interpersonal communication.
3. Success in business. 4. Publishers and publishing—Vocational
guidance. 5. Black, Cathie. I. Title. II. Title: Essential guide
for getting ahead at work (and in life).
HF5381.B448 2007
650.1—dc22 2007020752

ISBN 978-0-307-35110-4

Printed in the United States of America

DESIGN BY BARBARA STURMAN

10 9 8 7 6 5 4 3 2 1

First Edition

For Tom, Duffy, and Alison—
with love and affection

CONTENTS

Basic Black

Black on Black

My first job out of college, I thought I was a pretty hot property. I'd been hired at *Holiday* magazine in New York City, and was excited to have a real job, complete with a title: "sales assistant." For a young woman from the South Side of Chicago, it felt like the beginning of the glamorous life I'd dreamed of. Yet, exciting as it was, I was eager to move up quickly—so before long I was already angling for my next bigger, better job.

Then, one morning at work, my phone rang.

"Is this Cathleen P. Black?" asked a man on the other end of the line. I said it was.

"Cathleen P. Black, who lives at 215 East 80th Street, apartment 14F?" the man continued, the trace of a smirk in his voice. "A graduate of Trinity College in Washington, D.C., who is currently employed at *Holiday* magazine?"

My cheeks went hot. Whoever this guy was, he was reading

my résumé—which I'd polished up and made copies of the night before, after work.

"Who is this?" I asked.

"It's Harry Egner," he answered—a senior executive in the company! I started to stammer out an apology, but then I heard him laughing.

"Next time you're duplicating your résumé, Miss Black," he said, "I suggest you remember to take the original off the copier." I thanked him for the advice and hung up, shaking my head at how stupid my mistake had been—and how lucky I was that Harry Egner had gone so easy on me.

When I think of that story today, it reminds me not only of how green I was in my first job, but, more important, how little I realized that fact at the time. I didn't know what I didn't know, and in some ways that turned out to be helpful. But as I flew by the seat of my proverbial pants in those earlier years, I could really have benefited from some well-timed practical suggestions and advice.

That's what this book is about. As its title implies, it's full of simple, straightforward advice to help you not only navigate the world of work, but balance your work and personal life as well. Some of the suggestions are truly basic—commonsense observations that can produce real, immediate improvements in your work life. Others go deeper, exploring themes like ambition and self-confidence. Whether you're just starting out, moving up, or wanting to improve your management and leadership skills, there's something in here for you.

The book has three threads:

1. Chapters focus on the most important elements of life at work, illustrated with real-life stories. They offer a comprehensive look at keys to success—like drive, power, and passion.

2. Case Studies offer a deeper look at some real-life "teachable moments," and an inside peek at how legends of the corporate and media worlds—people like Oprah Winfrey and movie mogul Harvey Weinstein—do business.

3. Black & White sections offer straight-up practical tips, from how to run a meeting to the do's and don'ts of interviews. Whether they tell you something new or reinforce things you already know, Black & White tips offer concrete suggestions you can use every day.

But before I start giving you tips, I probably ought to answer one question: Who am I to be offering advice?

I've been lucky enough to work in the media business for my entire career, starting out with that advertising sales assistant job at *Holiday* magazine and ending up in my current position as president of Hearst Magazines, one of the world's largest publishers of monthly magazines, including *Cosmopolitan, Esquire, Harper's Bazaar,* and *O, the Oprah Winfrey Magazine.* Along the way, I've had the good fortune to work with some of the most colorful, fascinating people in media. Of course, I've also worked with my fair share of jerks, which makes for some fun stories in this book.

After spending a couple of years at *Holiday,* I began making my way up the advertising sales food chain. In my next two jobs I was a full-fledged ad sales representative—first at *Travel + Leisure* magazine, then at *New York* magazine, handling ever larger and more important accounts. I learned on the fly, making lots of mistakes and more than once inserting my foot firmly in my mouth, but with every sales call and deal made, I gained more confidence. I really liked sales and knew I was good at it, and after six years spent learning the advertising ropes, I felt ready for a new challenge. Good thing, too, because my next job definitely filled *that* bill.

I was hired as the advertising manager at a brand-new magazine called *Ms.* Though the word *groundbreaking* has been overused to the point of cliché, that's exactly what *Ms.* was: the first magazine for women that dared to venture beyond the "traditional" topics usually found in women's magazines. Co-founded by Gloria Steinem, the legendary icon of the feminist movement, *Ms.* was a pioneering editorial product, galvanizing a generation of women and shaping the national dialogue—but it was a hellishly hard sell for its advertising team.

As the Wikipedia entry for *Ms.* rather delicately puts it, the magazine "was not always able to reconcile its ideological concerns with commercial considerations." Translation: our ad sales team spent a lot of hours banging our heads against a wall, trying to win over skeptical advertisers. This new idea of "feminism" was hugely controversial, so whenever we showed up at potential advertisers' offices with our promotional materials (printed on hot pink paper), there was no telling whether they'd let us in, point us right back toward the door, or worse (as you'll hear about in a later chapter). Adversity is a great teacher, so I definitely learned a lot at *Ms.* Probably not coincidentally, it was also one of the most personally fulfilling jobs I've ever had.

After nearly a decade of living in New York City, though, I decided to pursue new adventures out west. The draw: a San Francisco–based magazine being started by film director Francis Ford Coppola. Sounds pretty sexy, right? A hip new weekly magazine started by the hottest director in Hollywood? I thought so, too—but within a few months of arriving in California, I realized the magazine wasn't going to work out quite as Coppola had envisioned. Not for the first time in history, and certainly not for the last, reality couldn't keep up with the hype. Lacking enough ads or circulation to succeed, the magazine folded after six months, so I turned around and headed back to New York City and *Ms.* magazine. Then, within a few years, my career took off when I was named publisher of *New York,* thereby becoming the first woman publisher of a weekly consumer magazine.

But hold on, enough about me—let's talk about you. Not everyone who enters the workforce (or buys a business book) does so with the goal of becoming a top executive, president, or CEO. You might want simply to succeed at your job with a minimum of stress and tension. You may be seeking advice on how to deal with a problem boss or employee. Perhaps you're looking for ways to maintain a happy personal life in addition to having fulfilling work. This book is aimed at helping *you* reach whatever *your* goal is, regardless of how ambitious you may be in the workplace.

In fact, one of the themes running through it is that age-old question of "having it all." After a decade in which that phrase became a buzzword, what does it really mean for you, today? Should you try to "have it all"—to climb the corporate ladder while simultaneously raising a family and having a life beyond the office? Or is it crazy to think you can do everything all at once? We'll explore the idea of creating what I call a "360° Life" for yourself—focusing on all aspects of day-to-day living, including work, relationships, home life, and family.

Finding the right answers starts with knowing which questions to ask. Throughout this book, we'll look at some of the important questions that can help you plan and shape your working life. For now, let's start with three basic ones.

- What are three problems you'd like to fix at your job?

- How much farther up the ladder can you see yourself in two years' time? How about in five years?

- What's that pie-in-the-sky goal you secretly dream about?

If you can't answer these right now, don't worry. Just keep them in mind, and the answers should become clearer as we go along. Remember, goals are easier to meet when they're clearly defined, so one of the things we'll be doing is helping you define your own personal goals.

The next step in my own career after *New York* magazine offers a great lesson in what can go wrong when you fail to define your terms in the workplace. I learned this the hard way, after starting my new job flying high—literally.

ONE morning in the fall of 1983, a stretch limousine glided to a stop in front of the offices of *New York* magazine. I walked out the building's front door and settled into the backseat for a short ride to La Guardia airport, where I was then escorted onto a private jet for a forty-five-minute flight to Washington, D.C.

I'd just been hired as the president of *USA Today,* which was then a fledgling daily newspaper, pummeled by critics and struggling to survive. Peering out the windows of the sleek Gulfstream jet, watching Manhattan recede into the distance, I suddenly felt a little dizzy at the realization of where I was and where I was going. They'd sent this entire jet just for me, complete with my own flight attendant! I'd never been on a corporate aircraft before, and as I stretched out my legs and gazed around the plush seats and upholstered interior, I felt like Dorothy gawking in wonder at the Land of Oz.

Unfortunately, that thrill would soon collapse with a thud. When the plane landed, another limo whisked me to *USA Today*'s towers on the banks of the Potomac River, where I was quickly ferried skyward. I emerged into a dining room packed with dozens of journalists, editors, and executives, all there for a special luncheon to introduce me as *USA Today*'s new president. The place was buzzing. The team had been toiling for a year to get the newspaper off the ground, and I was the third president to be named in that short time. I was also a female, non-newspaper person and an absolutely unknown quantity to these people—many of whom had just learned about my hiring moments beforehand. As I looked around the room, I could feel the questions in the air: Was I a savior, a marketing genius who could turn the paper around? Or would I be a flop?

It wasn't exactly like walking into a lion's den, but it was certainly nerve-wracking. And it became even more so when I greeted Joe Welty, a red-faced, heavyset advertising executive who appeared to be about fifteen years my senior. Joe brusquely shook my hand, barking a quick "Welcome to *USA Today*, Cathie." I started to thank him, but before I could get a word out, he pulled me aside and said, "I just want you to know up front, I'm not going to be reporting to you."

I stared at him, dumbfounded. Inside, I was seething. What did this mean? What in the world did the title "president" mean if key executives wouldn't be reporting to me? With a sick feeling, I realized I'd never nailed down, in writing, what my actual duties were to be. Here I was, all excited about my exalted new position—and title—but because I hadn't thought to work out the most important details in advance, I might possibly end up being little more than a figurehead. I couldn't believe that, this far into my career, I'd forgotten advice as basic as *Make sure your job responsibilities are clearly defined.*

All of which just goes to show that, at every level of your career, you can benefit from a refresher course on the basics. I'll reveal later in the book how that situation with Joe Welty was resolved, but for now let's just say that by ignoring one common-sense step, I added a whole new level of complication to my transition. These are the kinds of headaches I'd like to help you avoid.

To finish up with my short bio (and there is a happy ending), I spent eight fantastic years at *USA Today*. I then went on to head up the Newspaper Association of America for five years before accepting a position as president of Hearst Magazines, the position I hold today.

I've always loved working in the media business, because it's an industry of ideas and creative people, but this book isn't about the media. I've written it with a broader audience in mind—after all, much of the experience of what we call "work" is universal, and the best advice is the simple, common-denominator suggestions that apply across the board. So whether you work in media or in a corporate, nonprofit, or other environment, there are lessons and take-aways here that will apply to you.

BEFORE we get into the heart of the book, I can't resist telling one more story. When I first mentioned to Victor Ganzi, the president and CEO of the Hearst Corporation (and my boss) that I was writing a book, his reply was "It isn't going to be about Hearst, is it?" A privately held company, the Hearst Corporation has traditionally kept its inner workings to itself, and while Vic presumably knew I wasn't plotting some sort of exposé, he obviously thought it best to find out what exactly I planned to do.

I will, of course, write about some of my experiences at Hearst, as my time here has offered plenty of "teachable lessons," along with some inside stories of dealing with legends of American business. But I reassured Vic that no, I wasn't planning a whole book about the company. "In fact," I told him, "it's really more for your daughters." Twin sisters just turning thirty, one a lawyer and one a recent MBA, Vic's daughters are in the early stages of their journeys through the working world. I envisioned this book as a kind of tour guide to new terrain for them and others like them, regardless of age or level of achievement.

Okay, enough with the preliminaries—let's jump right into the real business of this book. Now that I've shared my two-minute personal employment history, perhaps we should start chapter 1 with a story about someone else: a young woman who wrote her way into magazine history with a tube of lipstick and a bold idea.

CHAPTER 1

Drive

One bright December morning, a young woman with a wild mane of black hair, tight jeans, four-inch stilettos, and feather earrings walked into my office at Hearst. Six feet tall, with a bombshell figure and striking dark eyes, she could have strutted right in like an Amazon. Yet I could see she was nervous—and why wouldn't she be? At age twenty-six, Atoosa Rubenstein, a fashion editor at *Cosmopolitan,* had come to pitch me on her idea for a new magazine.

It's pretty much unheard of in this business to give a twenty-something editor the chance to pitch a major new magazine directly to the president. But I'd heard about Atoosa's idea for launching a publication for teenage girls under the *Cosmopolitan* brand—she wanted to name it *CosmoGirl*—and I was intrigued. Born in Iran, raised in a conservative family, Atoosa sat in my office and talked with real passion about the pressures teenage girls face, the kind of advice and comfort they seek, and her vision for how to provide that in a monthly magazine.

I liked what I was hearing, and told her so.

"Well," she responded, "what would be the next step?"

"You should put together a prototype, or 'dummy,'" I said. "Go to the newsstand, buy a bunch of magazines, and cut and paste them together into the kind of magazine you envision. Don't go hire an art director on the side—this should be *your* vision and passion. Bring it to me when it's ready."

Atoosa didn't hesitate. "When would you like to see it?"

"Sooner's always better than later," I told her. And with that, our meeting ended. Like a gangly teenager, Atoosa bounded out of my office with a good-bye wave, excited to get started.

Now, to be honest, Atoosa wasn't exactly breaking the mold by pitching a magazine aimed at teenage girls—any glance at a grocery store magazine rack will show you that. In fact, we'd been discussing the possibility of starting a teen magazine at Hearst well before Atoosa made her pitch. But there were other things that set Atoosa, and her presentation, apart. For one thing, it was clear right away that she had a real emotional connection to teenage girls—she knew and remembered well their angst, insecurities, and hopes. But, more important, she had demonstrated the single most important element she'd need to succeed in her quest: **drive.**

Atoosa had demonstrated this in three ways:

- She planted the seed for getting a meeting with me by telling her boss, *Cosmopolitan* editor-in-chief Kate White, about her magazine idea.

- Once in the meeting, not only did she communicate real passion for her subject, but she took it a step further by asking me what her next move should be.

- She asked for a specific deadline, so she could get me her prototype when I wanted it.

All this was good, and I took notice. But then Atoosa took it to an even higher level.

After our meeting, she went straight to a newsstand and bought dozens of magazines, took them home, and started cutting them up like crazy. She planted herself in her bedroom, surrounded by hundreds of clippings covering the bed, floor, and tables, and began gluing pages together left and right. She wrote the name "CosmoGirl" over and over in twenty-seven different shades of lipstick, trying to capture just the right youthful image, until she fell asleep exhausted, the lipsticks permanently staining her new white bedspread (to the chagrin of her new husband).

Over the course of forty-eight hours, Atoosa hardly slept at all, determined as she was to get her dummy finished by the close of business on Friday afternoon. She'd found out from my assistant that I was scheduled to leave the office at five-thirty, and she was anxious for me to have it for the weekend. Then, just as she was ready to print out the final pages, the inevitable glitch happened—the printer in her office went down. She watched in dismay as the clock ticked past her self-imposed deadline.

When the machine was back up and running, she printed out the final version. Disappointed at missing her chance to get it to me for the weekend, she asked her assistant to call my office. By then she figured she'd just send it over via interoffice mail, and I'd get it on Monday. But, to her surprise, I hadn't left yet. "Why don't you come over now," I told her, "and show me what you've got."

Though the *Cosmopolitan* offices were a five-minute walk away, Atoosa arrived breathless about two and a half minutes after she hung up the phone. She walked in, handed me the dummy, and began excitedly telling me about what she'd done.

"Slow down," I told her. "I'm not going anywhere." And indeed I wasn't. I was too busy flipping through the prototype of what I already knew would be Hearst's next new magazine.

It was fantastic—so full of energy and feeling, and different from other teen magazines in that it had Atoosa's personal, more emotional touch. She had, in her own words, been the classic "ugly duckling" growing up, a gawky, uncertain girl with constellations of pimples and a lingering sense of being the geek. The magazine she envisioned was what she had craved herself as a teenager. For her, *CosmoGirl* would be more than a magazine—it would be a mission. She would be the "big sister."

I put the dummy up on a display shelf in my office, along with the latest issues of all of Hearst's magazines, from *Cosmopolitan* to *Harper's Bazaar* to *Marie Claire* to *Esquire* and *Popular Mechanics*. "Atoosa," I said, "it looks like we might have ourselves a magazine." Later she'd tell me she didn't know for sure what that meant—was she to be the editor? Or would Hearst take her creative idea and pick someone more experienced? That would have been crushing, but at least she knew that whatever the case, her magazine would become a reality. And she was so excited that when she reached to shake my hand, she grabbed my wrist instead, eagerly pumping it up and down.

The American Heritage Dictionary defines drive in two ways:

- *a strong, organized effort to accomplish a purpose*

- *energy, push, or aggressiveness*

Here's how I define it: doing whatever it takes to propel yourself to the next level, whether it's aiming for a big promotion, looking for a new job, accepting a transfer, starting a whole new career, or just figuring out the next step in a project. Drive is the act of moving forward on your own initiative, and it's one of the most important traits to have if you want to succeed in your work and in life.

Yet you don't have to pitch a whole new business idea, magazine, or TV show like Atoosa did to prove you've got drive. At its most basic level, drive involves being motivated enough to track down information you need for tasks ahead, so you don't make obvious mistakes. It's as simple as this:

> Make like a Boy Scout: Be prepared!

If you're well prepared for meetings, presentations, or just everyday work tasks, you're far more likely to advance in your job. If you aren't, not only will you thwart your own progress, but you'll almost certainly end up making embarrassing mistakes.

Here's a perfect example: When I was just out of college, working at *Holiday* magazine, I had a roommate who worked as the assistant to the cartoon editor at another magazine. She'd been there about a week, and one evening when she came back to our apartment, we got to talking about our days, what we'd done, and different aspects of our jobs, including sending out correspondence.

"My boss writes his letters on a yellow legal pad," she told me.

"Can you read his writing?" I asked.

"Why?"

"Well," I said, "deciphering someone's handwriting to type a letter is always so hard."

She looked at me blankly. "I don't type them," she said. "I just fold them, stick them in envelopes, and send them out."

Now, I was pretty inexperienced myself at that point, but I knew that sending out hand-scrawled letters on yellow lined paper just couldn't be right. "I don't think that's what your boss had in mind," I said. "I'm pretty sure he's expecting to get those back, typed, so he can sign them."

Her face went pale. "Oh my God!" she shrieked. "He never told me that!"

Well, no, he didn't—because it wasn't his job to make sure she understood the basics of her duties. That story's funny now, but I guarantee it wasn't funny for my roommate when she went to work the next day and had to tell her boss what she'd been doing. In any work environment, it's essential to know what's expected—the do's, the don'ts, and the don't-forgets. And if there's anything you're unsure of,

> **Ask someone who knows.**

The act of asking is one of the most important elements of success. All too often, people fear that asking questions reveals ignorance, yet the opposite is true. The root of the word *ignorance,* after all, is *ignore.* The minute you ask about something, you've taken a step toward understanding it. On the other hand, if you just ignore the fact that you don't know—believe me, you won't get away with that for long.

There's another, less obvious benefit to being the most prepared person in a room. Not only will you know what the hell you're doing, but others—your boss, colleagues, clients, customers, and even competitors—will take note of it and perceive you differently. Sometimes that can be the most important thing, as this next story shows.

One morning during my time at *USA Today,* we had a meeting scheduled with an advertising agency that was trying to win our account. At that time, in the early startup years, we were spending money like crazy trying to promote the paper. So landing our account would be a huge, lucrative "get" for whichever agency won it.

Just before the meeting was to start, I walked out to the reception area to greet the ad agency's senior account guy. He was sitting on a couch, flipping idly through that morning's copy of *USA Today.* When he saw me, he tossed the paper down on the coffee table, said something like "Well, that's a nice quick read," and got up to shake my hand. All I could think was *You idiot. There's no way you're getting our account.*

This guy had come to pitch us on representing our product—yet he hadn't even bothered to read that morning's paper until he could grab a free copy in our reception area? To be truly prepared, he should have devoured at least the last two weeks' worth of issues, as well as those of our biggest competitors. How in the world could he know what set *USA Today* apart from other newspapers if he hadn't bothered to read it? And if he didn't know, then how could he possibly communicate it to others? Was he, and by extension his agency, someone we could trust to create the right brand image for our newspaper? In that first minute, I already knew the answer was no.

Making sure you've prepared yourself with the information you need is Step One. Making doubly sure that that information is correct is Step Two, and no less important. Remember to

> **Check and double-check (then check again,**
> **if you're still not sure).**

There's an old saying among journalists: "If your mother says she loves you, check it." And in fact you can be sure that the minute you take something for granted, it won't be what you thought it was. Take my name, for example. When I was in junior high, a skinny, awkward preteen with big dreams, I decided I wanted to be different, so one day I changed the spelling of my name from "Cathy" to "Cathie." Silly, I know—but what can I say? When you're twelve, these kinds of things seem desperately important.

I can't tell you how many times over the years I've received letters addressed to "Cathy Black," or "Kathy Black," or "Kathleen Black." It seems like a little deal, but it's a big deal to me—and it's the quickest way to lower my opinion of the letter writer. After all, it takes about five seconds to go online or call Hearst and find out how my name is spelled and my exact title. Anyone who can't spare that little bit of time to avoid making a basic mistake has really damaged her chances. Don't let little, easily corrected mistakes ruin your chances for getting a job, winning an account, or being taken seriously before you can even state your case.

Showing drive, and persistence, during the hiring process is the best way to improve your chances of landing that big interview or dream job. Yet for some reason people often choose the most passive route possible when pursuing a new job. Do you ever

- send out a letter and résumé and wait (in vain) for someone to call you?

- assume you shouldn't call to follow up, because, well, they'll call if they want to talk to you?

- choose not to ask someone for help getting your foot in the door somewhere, because you want to do it on your own terms?

If you've done any of the above, you're certainly not alone; they're all-too-common mistakes. But what better way to get on an employer's radar screen than a follow-up call, which in one swoop demonstrates pluck, initiative, interest, and drive? Sitting back and waiting for someone to call you shows the opposite. So don't be afraid to

---

Pick up that phone.

Believe me, employers are *not* turned off when you call and politely inquire whether your résumé was received. And they honestly don't mind if you then take that opportunity to reiterate how interested you are in the position. If nothing else, the fact that you called will differentiate you from the mob of other candidates who are applying.

If you've ever worked in an office, you know the kinds of things that go on. Correspondence is misplaced. Meetings pile up. Deadlines slide. When you send a résumé and don't hear anything back immediately, chances are good that it has nothing to do with you. So take a minute and make that call—it can't hurt, and it certainly might help. (For more tips on résumés, interviews, and follow-ups, check out the Black & White section called "Landing Your Dream Job" later in this book.)

In that same vein, don't be afraid to call and ask friends, colleagues, former bosses—anyone who might have clout—for help in securing a job interview. What's the worst thing that can happen? That someone can't (or, very rarely, would rather not) help you—in which case you haven't lost anything. More often than not, seeking a little inside help is the smartest, quickest way to get access to the person who might be able to hire you.

Early one morning when I was working at *Ms.* magazine, I made a call to George Hirsch, my former boss and the former publisher of *New York* magazine. I hadn't worked for George in several years, but I'd made a point of keeping in touch and asking his advice from time to time. That morning I called him at home before going to the office, with a very specific request.

"Can we get together?" I asked him. "There's something I need to talk with you about."

"Well," George said, "I'm going out of town today. Can we do it when I get back?"

The polite thing, of course, would have been to say, "Sure, George. Have a great trip," and let him go on his way. Instead, I said, "Can you meet with me before you leave? How about if we grab a quick cup of coffee, or breakfast?"

George, who is not only a legend in the magazine world but also one of the smartest, most thoughtful people I've ever met, could hear the urgency in my voice. "Okay," he said. "Where?"

A half hour later, George and I were ensconced in a booth at a diner, ordering eggs and coffee. "I have a favor to ask," I told him, and took a deep breath. "Can you introduce me to Francis Ford Coppola?"

Now, a little background is in order here. I'd recently heard that movie director Francis Ford Coppola was branching out from his film interests to launch a new magazine in San Francisco— news that came just as I was nearing a point, both personally and professionally, when I wanted a change. I'd spent the previous decade in New York City, and though I loved my work and life, my marriage was ending and I wanted to make a fresh start. On a recent trip to San Francisco, I had found myself completely enchanted by the city. Surprisingly quickly, I decided I wanted to move there.

Getting a job with Coppola's new magazine would be the perfect way to relocate—having a great job already in hand, and with a major media figure to boot. And because I knew that George Hirsch knew Coppola, my next step was clear. Of course, I could have insisted on doing it without help, but why? George could get me in the door quickly, and the fact that Coppola knew and trusted him would work in my favor.

George didn't hesitate. "Of course," he told me. "Let me give him a call." As it turned out, Coppola was in New York that day, and within a few hours I was on my way to meet with him at a large suite in the elegant Pierre Hotel on Fifth Avenue. A couple of days later I had an actual job offer. The truth is, if I'd relied only on myself, I'd probably have never gotten through his gate-keepers to set up that initial meeting.

So don't be shy about using your contacts. Most people are flattered when you ask for help. Friends and former employees have asked me for help many times over the years, and I can tell you it just feels good to help someone whose skills and reputation you believe in. And besides, it can be good business. After all, if I recommend you for a job, and you turn out to be a great hire, I've earned a chit with your new employer. Doing someone else a favor can, in many ways, be just as beneficial as having one done for you.

But what should you do if you don't have those contacts to help you get in the door? Well, you could do what a young woman named Bonnie Fuller did early in her career, when she wanted to get the attention of the legendary *Cosmopolitan* magazine editor Helen Gurley Brown:

> **Sell yourself as though you believe in the product.**

In the late 1980s, Helen Gurley Brown was in her third decade of editing *Cosmopolitan* magazine, which she'd transformed from a moribund monthly into one of the most successful magazines for young women in history. The author of *Sex and the Single Girl,* the manifesto that kick-started the women's sexual revolution, Helen (who still works for Hearst as the editor-in-chief of *Cosmopolitan*'s international editions) was a bona fide celebrity. With her short Pucci skirts, purring voice, and trademark pouf of perfectly coiffed hair, Helen was as famous as they come in the magazine world. And she loved every bit of it.

Bonnie Fuller, on the other hand, was the unknown young editor of a Canadian fashion magazine called *Flare.* She hadn't come from a wealthy family and didn't have many contacts in the New York magazine world, but the one thing she had in overstock was drive. And because Canada is not exactly center stage in the world of fashion, Bonnie was determined to go where the action was.

Not having an easy "in" to the rarefied world of Helen Gurley Brown, Bonnie took it upon herself to send, unsolicited, a copy of her magazine to Helen—and to a number of other top magazine editors as well.

Every month.

For several years.

She'd write a short note—"Just thought you'd like to see the March issue!"—then stick it in an envelope and mail it. She never asked whether Helen wanted to receive the magazine, or even whether she looked at it or not. Bonnie simply believed enough in herself to put it out there. She didn't badger or provoke. She didn't make twenty-three calls in one week to demand a response. She simply took action to make sure she was noticed. And Helen definitely noticed.

By 1994, Bonnie had landed herself a job at Hearst as the editor of *Marie Claire,* a plum job in the world of fashion magazines. And three years after that, just as I was coming to Hearst, she took on the most exciting job in the magazine business— following in the footsteps of Helen Gurley Brown herself as the first new editor of *Cosmopolitan* magazine in thirty years. Bonnie's rise makes for an amazing story, and it never would have happened if she hadn't taken the initiative in selling herself.

After all, if *you* don't sell yourself, who will?

PREPARING ferociously and selling yourself are key ways of showing drive, but the way to become great—and advance accordingly—is to make it a habit to push even farther, and do the unexpected. So:

> Go that extra mile, or even a mile and a half.

Anyone can go the extra mile: interns looking for a summer job, assistants hoping to advance into a more senior position, company executives seeking to maintain good relations with clients and customers. Whatever your position is, try to make a habit of taking the next step or two beyond what you've been asked to do. Your efforts will more than pay off in the end.

A couple of years ago, an article in one of Hearst's magazines, *House Beautiful,* misidentified the owner of a certain Aspen home as the "chairman of the Estée Lauder Companies," Ronald Lauder, and "his wife Evelyn." Unfortunately, Ronald isn't the chairman of Lauder, nor is Evelyn his wife. The article was referring to Ronald's *brother,* the legendary Leonard Lauder, who is very well known in New York—in circles from art to media to philanthropy, and who is married to Evelyn.

Arrgh! It was an innocent mistake, but an incredibly stupid one, and once I was told about it, I knew we needed to 'fess up immediately. The Lauder companies, which spend many tens of millions annually on advertising and promotion, are a major advertiser in our magazines. I couldn't take the chance that our blunder would leave a bad taste in their chairman's mouth. And since I'd known Leonard Lauder for years, I wanted to apologize to him personally.

It was a Friday before a holiday weekend. I got on the phone to Leonard's office and learned from his assistant that he and Evelyn were traveling in France. He would have no idea yet about the error, so now was my chance to get to him before he heard about it from his public relations department. Hearing my desperation, the assistant gave me the number of his hotel in Paris.

I told him about the mistake. "Leonard, I'm sorry," I said. "And more than that, I'm embarrassed."

Leonard laughed and told me all was forgiven. He passed the phone to Evelyn, who was also very gracious. And as he later told an interviewer for a magazine article profiling me, he was pleased I'd gone to the trouble of tracking him down to apologize. "My regard for her," he said, "shot up into the stratosphere." By going the extra mile, I'd managed not only to head off any ill effects of the mistake, but to turn it into a net plus.

Often, what clients and customers really want is a simple acknowledgment that someone is looking out for them. At *USA Today* I got into the habit of calling major advertisers if an unflattering story about their product appeared in the newspaper. Once a full-page four-color ad for Dewar's scotch ended up next to a story about alcoholism and its negative impact on the American economy. Another time, Toys "R" Us had bought significant ad space for the same day the paper covered the Consumer Product Safety Commission's report on dangerous toys.

It's the newspaper's responsibility to report the news, of course, so I didn't have any problem with that. But it was my responsibility to make sure our advertisers weren't upset with us about possible collateral damage to their companies or their products. So I made a point of calling to smooth ruffled feathers, or even hopping on a plane to visit the advertiser, going that extra mile (literally!) to make things right.

Once, however, on a day when Chrysler ran a full-page, four-color ad, I hardly had time to react. I'd just gotten into the office and as I flipped to the automotive page, I saw that our reporter had harshly criticized one of Chrysler's cars in his "best and worst new models" ratings. *Uh-oh,* I thought. And just at that moment my phone rang.

It was Lee Iacocca, the chairman of Chrysler and the man who'd gained fame for turning the ailing company around. He was livid, and let me know in a raving tirade of colorful language exactly what he thought about our automotive reporter, our newspaper, and, for good measure, our obvious intellectual deficiencies. Somehow I knew that all Iacocca really wanted was to vent—he was probably showing off for people in his office at that moment—so I took the time to act as a willing ear, then offered a few soothing words before he slammed the phone down. Chrysler wasn't going to stop advertising in *USA Today*, and Iacocca certainly couldn't demand that we skew our automotive reports to please him.

Having a reputation for making the extra effort is a great way to get noticed. And going that extra mile for yourself can also be lucrative. I discovered that personally when I took the time to

> **Pluck the presidential tomato.**

One rainy morning during my tenure as *New York* magazine's publisher, I was out at our weekend cottage in Connecticut, working on my hands and knees in the garden. Dressed in cutoff shorts and a T-shirt, a shower cap on my head to protect my hair, I was clawing through the dirt with abandon when I looked up to see a black stretch limo pulling into our driveway.

The driver got out and pulled out a gargantuan basket of herbs from the specialty grocery store Dean & DeLuca, along with a bottle of Dom Perignon. I looked at him in surprise, sweating under my shower cap. "These are for you," he said.

I carried the basket into the house and pulled out the card. It was from Al Neuharth, the chairman and CEO of the Gannett Company, one of the largest newspaper publishers in the country. At the time Neuharth was trying to persuade me to take a corporate marketing job with Gannett, but so far I hadn't bitten—the job he had in mind just wasn't the right fit. I was intrigued by the idea of working for Gannett's newest venture, *USA Today,* but Neuharth hadn't suggested anything there, so it appeared we were at a stalemate.

Still, Neuharth always managed to keep our conversation going with yet another meeting or dinner, and we'd been engaged in a cat-and-mouse game for several months now. The basket of herbs and champagne, which also contained a copy of Gannett's most recent annual report, was his way of saying, "Let's give this one more go, to see if we can find the right job for you."

I was impressed and amused by Neuharth's grand gesture. I also found it stoked a competitive fire in me. I decided it would be fun to one-up him, and fortunately I already had the perfect vehicle for doing so. The day before, I'd plucked a gigantic tomato off one of our vines—I mean this thing was a monster, a real Frankenstein vegetable. It must have been six inches across. I had never before grown a tomato that large, and doubted I ever would again. So when I agreed to meet with Neuharth and other executives later in the week, I decided to bring it along as a gift.

I packed the tomato in crinkly tissue paper, nestled it in a box, and put a blue ribbon on top, as if it were the winning entry at the county fair. At our meeting—over dinner at the swanky Four Seasons restaurant—I presented it with great fanfare. "Al," I announced, "I know you don't believe I've ever spent a minute in a garden, but I grew this especially for you." When he opened the box, everyone at the table cracked up. No one could believe I'd grown it, or that I'd actually brought a giant vegetable as a gift to the chairman of a $2-billion company.

Later in the evening, after most of the group had left, Gannett's senior vice-president of human resources, Madelyn Jennings, asked me the question I'd been waiting to hear. "What do you really want to do at Gannett?" she said.

"Well, the place that makes the most sense is *USA Today,*"

I told her. "But I know the positions of president and publisher are filled, and those are the only titles I'd go for."

And that was that. One week later, Neuharth invited me to his New York suite at the Waldorf Towers. After a few minutes of polite chitchat, he offered me the position of president of *USA Today*, saying he'd shuffled around a few titles to open it up. "You could have saved yourself a lot of fancy dinners if you'd just offered that to begin with," I told him with a smile as we shook hands.

I didn't get offered that job just because of the giant tomato, of course. But I could tell from the beginning that Neuharth was the kind of guy who'd respond well to a confident riposte. Odd as it may sound, it showed him I was up for the game, sure enough of myself to engage him in a bold, unusual way. And I do believe it was the tipping point that made him determined to find a way to hire me—even if it meant moving other people around to make it happen. So ever since that day, I've thought of it as my Presidential Tomato.

I felt pretty good about my tomato idea—and, more important, I was thrilled with my new job and title. Yet as clever as I may have felt, I soon found that Al Neuharth had planned an even more clever trick of his own. And I learned it the hard way, because I failed to go the extra mile in one very important respect, forgetting to

---

Assume nothing.

In the prologue to this book, I wrote about my rude awakening to the fact that my new title, "president," didn't mean what I thought it did. When advertising executive Joe Welty announced brusquely that he wouldn't be reporting to me, I suddenly realized that I'd never nailed down the reporting structure or what my actual duties were. Talk about flying high and coming down with a crash! I'd made a classic—and easily avoidable—mistake.

My embarrassment quickly passed, though, replaced with a desire to put Welty—who had, after all, made a choice to undermine my authority aggressively from our very first hello—back in his place. Luckily, I had my opportunity at the end of the luncheon. Welty and I were both scheduled to return to New York. "Cathie, you take the corporate jet," Neuharth's assistant Randy Chorney told me, before turning to Welty. "Joe," she said, "you take the shuttle." I'll admit to a pleasant feeling of vindication as I watched Welty's eyes narrow and his face redden. And though it might sound trivial, this wasn't about the plane. It was about establishing quickly that my position represented more than an empty title.

Al Neuharth, of course, had kept my duties vague on purpose. He knew I'd come to *USA Today* only if I could be its president, but he also had seasoned executives in place who had more experience than I did in many elements of a big newspaper president's job. So he played it both ways, giving me the title I wanted without cutting the legs out from underneath the others.

As I'd soon discover, this was typical Al Neuharth—cunning, manipulative, and aimed at getting what he wanted. He'd duped me, and that was my own fault. But now I was determined to do two things: first, to take over the responsibilities I had assumed would be mine, even if it took months; and, second, never again to be surprised like that.

SURPRISES are fun in some contexts, but almost never at work—which brings us to three more ways to show drive:

- Never surprise your boss.

- Anticipate his or her needs.

- Make him or her look good.

Ultimately, your boss is the person with the biggest say in whether or not you advance. In any company or organization, there are others who can help you, too—vice-presidents who'll put in a good word, or board members you've impressed—but it's your immediate supervisor whose assessment will carry the most weight. So why not go out of your way to make sure he or she in particular is satisfied with your work?

Let's start with *anticipation*. It's good to respond quickly and efficiently when your boss asks you for something. But what if you pushed that one step further and provided it before your boss even asked? No one's suggesting you become a mind-reader, but it's often not difficult to figure out the next thing your boss needs. Sometimes it's just a question of reading his body language.

Recently I was in a meeting with our CEO and a very talented executive in our company. The executive was reviewing a plan for a big event, but as I watched the CEO squirm ever so slightly, I could see something was making him uncomfortable. I stepped in and suggested a compromise, but really what I was thinking was, *I need to make sure this gets resolved in a way he likes.* Anytime I can find a way to take pressure off my boss, that's my number-one focus until it's accomplished. If I can find a way to do it that saves face for the others involved, so much the better.

Figure out the constituency you need to satisfy. If you work in a small organization, perhaps it's the head of your department. If you work in a nonprofit, perhaps it's the board. If you're a freelancer, perhaps it's the agent who can get you your next job. Even Donald Graham, the son of Katharine Graham and successor to her position atop the Washington Post Company, routinely made time for long walks with the top executives when he was publisher of the newspaper. He went out of his way to make sure the people most responsible for the paper's content felt that they were being heard.

Once you know *whom* you need to satisfy, find out exactly *how* to do it. If you've never asked your boss how she'd prefer to work with you, make a point of doing that. Ask basic questions like these:

- How often would you like to meet for project updates? Do you want interim reports by email?

- Do you prefer project reports as spreadsheets, or summarized in memo form?

- Do you want to see relevant correspondence on a project, or do you prefer getting a general summary from me?

These things may seem small, but taking the time to learn your boss's preferences can pay off big. It's like being in a hotel where all the small touches are done right—chocolates on the pillow, fluffy towels. The overall experience is greatly enhanced. Make sure you're enhancing your boss's work life as much as you can.

Remember, too, that this includes learning what your boss *doesn't* need from you. When Atoosa Rubenstein became editor of *CosmoGirl,* she jumped up the hierarchy at Hearst. At *Cosmo* she had reported to the editor, Kate White. Now she reported directly to me. Young and inexperienced, Atoosa continued to act in ways more befitting a midlevel staffer than editor-in-chief.

When she was reporting to Kate White, she made a point of sending quick emails to let Kate know when she was leaving the building or out of contact. And for the first week or so after her big promotion, she did the same with me: "I'm going to get lunch, be back in an hour," or "I'm going to an appointment— call me if you need me." What she didn't realize was that I had no need to receive all these messages—she'd progressed past the point of having to check in constantly with her superior. I'd just glance at her emails, chuckle, and delete them, but before I had a chance to tell her to stop sending them, she apparently realized herself that they were unnecessary. I never got another one.

You want to look good to your boss, of course, but don't forget the corollary:

Make your boss look good.

When I saw the movie *The Devil Wears Prada,* a scene that stuck in my head was the one in which Miranda Priestly's assistant, Andy, stood behind her boss's shoulder at a party, whispering the names of guests as they approached. As smooth as satin, Miranda greeted each person, coming off as an attentive and caring hostess rather than as the frosty, bored snob she really was.

There's no quicker, easier way to earn your boss's respect and gratitude than by helping her look good. When you're working for someone, it's sometimes easy to forget that she's working for another person higher up the chain, and she's every bit as concerned as you are with impressing her superiors. Whatever you can do to help her will pay off handsomely.

After I'd been at *USA Today* for nearly two years, I was in desperate need of a vacation. Al Neuharth wasn't keen on my taking two weeks off, but my husband and I rented a small flat in the south of France anyway (more about this in chapter 7). When we got there, we promptly found ourselves completely out of contact with the rest of the world—no phone, no fax, no email. I was proud of myself for having insisted on my vacation time, but this wasn't quite what I'd bargained for. If something went wrong and the office needed to reach me, there was no way they could easily do it.

When I came back to work two weeks later, tanned, rested, and slightly anxious about how things had gone in my absence,

I learned that our advertising director, Valerie Salembier, had vouched for me in the midst of a mini-crisis. Neuharth had demanded to know whether I was keeping in touch while I was away, and she had responded brightly, "I talk to her every other day. Everything's in control." Big smile.

Yes, she flat-out lied for me. And no, I'm not necessarily advocating lying as an office strategy. But in this case Valerie weighed whether any serious harm could come of covering for me, and made her decision accordingly. She knew I'd benefit from her decision, and by extension, so would she. And believe me, she was right—I never forgot that display of loyalty.

Finally, never surprise your boss. If you've got bad news, tell it. If you've got good news, share it. For one thing, no one likes to feel out of the loop. And for another, hiding a crisis from someone who needs to know virtually guarantees the problem will be compounded. Think of your boss as a small woodland animal—make no startling moves or strange gestures.

That's something I definitely didn't do in one infamous episode with Al Neuharth. It was one of my most embarrassing moments on the job at *USA Today,* a slipup I never should have committed, involving an airplane, a plate of barbecued ribs, and a notoriously fastidious personality. Read on for the whole smelly story.

Don't Take No for an Answer: Al Neuharth

In my first year at *USA Today,* I was airborne so much, I felt as if I might sprout wings. The newspaper had just launched, and part of my team's job was to jet around the country, often with Al Neuharth, to pitch the paper and try to drum up ad sales.

Whether for meetings, receptions, or dinners, our schedule was always tight. We'd fly into a city, take a car straight to our destination, and spend the next couple of hours trying to win over the potential advertiser. Neuharth would do the "soft sell," explaining how *USA Today* was a different kind of newspaper and extolling its mass appeal, and then I'd move in for the kill, angling for a commitment to buy ads. Even at dinners and receptions, it was nearly impossible to eat, as we had a limited time to make our sale, and pitching someone with one's mouth full of salad is less than effective.

We'd usually get back to the airport tired and hungry, and though the plane usually had a stocked bar and food, this time we hatched what we thought was a brilliant plan. "Isn't Kansas City famous for barbecued ribs?" someone asked as the plane touched down. "Why don't we get the limo driver to pick some up for us while we're at the reception?"

Well, that sounded perfect. We'd be starving by the time we got back to the airport, so why not treat ourselves to a local specialty for the flight back?

Neuharth didn't hear our conversation, so he didn't learn of our barbecue feast until we all returned to the airport at the end of the day, carrying big bags of pungent ribs up the steps into the plane. Into *his* plane. Into the *immaculate, white-leather interior* of his beloved Gulfstream. Hmm . . . putting it that way, I guess I should have foreseen what came next.

We dug into those ribs with abandon, eating like there was no tomorrow. It was a perfect barbecue feast, with tangy sauce, cold beer, and plenty of noisy finger-licking. We weren't eating like savages—there wasn't barbecue sauce flying all over the plane's interior—but we were, shall we say, completely into the moment.

Just then, Neuharth poked his head out of his private cabin in the rear of the plane, where he liked to work or rest during flights. He peered around briefly, with an odd look on his face, then shut the door. We didn't see him again for the rest of the flight. But his assistant, Randy Chorney, remarked, "I don't think Al's happy. He seems to be in a bad mood." Nothing more came of it, and by the time the plane landed back in New York, we'd cleaned up the remnants of our dinner and were all ready to head home for a well-earned sleep.

The next morning, Neuharth called me. "Meet me tonight at 5:00 p.m. at the Sky Club," he said—a private dining club in a Park Avenue skyscraper.

"Sure," I replied. "What's up?"

"Just be there," he said.

Neuharth had never invited me to meet him for a drink before, so I knew something was going on. I got to the club, met him at his table, and barely had time to settle in my chair before he leaned over and let me have it.

"Who in God's name had the idea of bringing those greasy, stinking barbecued ribs to mess up my airplane?" he demanded, his eyes flashing with irritation.

Whoops. I looked at him in surprise, then decided in an instant there was only one way to respond.

"It was mine, Al," I said. "And you know, I just wasn't thinking. It never occurred to me that having the ribs on board might bother you. But it's not my plane—it's your plane. And I'm sorry." I could have defended myself, but that would only have compounded the problem. My boss was unhappy as a direct result of a decision I'd made, so the best thing to do was to fix it: *Make your boss happy.* (And, for God's sake, know what might make him really *unhappy,* too.)

As it turned out, Neuharth had sat fuming in his private cabin the whole trip back. You could argue, of course, that his anger was out of proportion. After all, we did clean up after ourselves, and the plane's interior didn't have a drop of stray barbecue sauce on it. But Neuharth is a fastidious man. It's one of his many defining traits, some of which were simply odd—and some of which made him one of the most effective people I've ever worked with.

It's worth painting a fuller portrait of Neuharth, because he's not only a fascinating guy, but a real pro at marketing. I learned so much from him through the years—lessons that have continued to help me throughout my career. Of all of them, the most important was one that could serve as Neuharth's mantra:

Don't take no for an answer.

There's an old physics riddle that asks, "What happens when an irresistible force meets an immovable object?" We discovered the answer to that question in those early days of *USA Today*.

Al Neuharth was the irresistible force. Raised on a farm by his widowed mother in South Dakota, Neuharth was absolutely driven to succeed. After majoring in journalism at the University of South Dakota, he worked for two years as an Associated Press reporter before launching his own weekly tabloid, *SoDak Sports*. This was a bold venture for a young man in his twenties, and in the beginning it was successful. But after two years the fledgling newspaper folded. Undaunted, Neuharth took a job as a reporter for the *Miami Herald* and moved to Florida.

Within seven years Neuharth had worked his way up to assistant managing editor at the *Herald.* He then switched to the *Detroit Free Press,* working his way up to the top tier of editors before joining the Gannett Company in 1963 as the general manager of its two newspapers in Rochester, New York. Neuharth was an able manager, but at heart he was an entrepreneur. And at Gannett he was now able to indulge that entrepreneurial side, starting with a new paper in northern Florida.

Neuharth had discovered that no daily newspaper served Florida's "space coast"—the area between Palm Beach and Jacksonville that was home to Cape Canaveral and its highly educated employees and contractors. So Neuharth started a daily paper named *Today,* which was later renamed *Florida Today.* The paper was a success, but it was merely the precursor to Neuharth's grand idea, hatched in 1979 when he'd risen to become chairman and CEO of Gannett. He wanted to start a national daily newspaper—something no one had ever attempted before. He decided to call it *USA Today.*

From the beginning, skeptics saw this as an impossibly huge undertaking—printing and distributing a four-color newspaper that would be available every weekday morning *across the entire country*? How could that be anything but a pipe dream? But where most people saw only obstacles, Neuharth saw opportunities. He pioneered the use of color at a time when all newspapers were in black and white and a color front page was truly startling. And he knew that new technology would allow Gannett to send newspaper content via satellite to local printing plants, which would make it possible to insert very late-breaking news and sports scores into the paper. As a sports fanatic, Neuharth saw a market there. In those pre-Internet days, sports fans would be able to get their favorite teams' scores and game coverage, no matter where they were in the country.

Still, people thought Neuharth was crazy—but it was a perception he seemed to enjoy. He'd always been an outsider in the clubby world of the newspaper elite, and he played up the role. Dressed in sleek silk suits, with an ever-present pair of dark aviator glasses, he'd have fit in at a Las Vegas casino. He wore a gemstone-encrusted ring so big it could have served as brass knuckles in a fight. (For all I know, it did once or twice.) And while the New York media elite typically rode around in black Lincoln Town Cars, he tooled around in a white stretch limousine.

Neuharth was a man of many quirks. In restaurants, like some kind of mafioso, he refused to sit with his back to the door. He typed notes to colleagues and employees on his old Royal typewriter, on special peach-colored paper. And he loved placing bets on whatever popped into his head. At a football game he'd bet not only on the score, but on whether the singer performing "The Star-Spangled Banner" would hit that super-high note on the word *free.* If anyone failed to pay up after losing a bet (typical amounts ranged from five to ten dollars), Neuharth would send out a dunning notice within three days—no matter whether they were a friend, employee, or advertiser.

Oddest of all, Neuharth chose to keep his home base not in New York and not in Washington, D.C., but in the sleepy town of Cocoa Beach, Florida. He did this for a reason: he wanted to create a new paper that would turn the dynamic of the newspaper business upside-down, and he wanted to do it far from the peering eyes of the critics. Neuharth didn't want their scrutiny, and he didn't want the editors and reporters to be locked in to the New York media world, as he felt there was a biased view of news. "You know," he told me once, "these snobby New York newspaper editors live in their ivory towers, preaching down to the world about what they think is important. But *USA Today* is a reader's newspaper. We cover the things people care most about—the things that affect their communities, their interests, their families, and their jobs."

Because *USA Today* is so successful now, it's hard to remember that in the beginning almost everyone expected it to fail. Media critics mocked its simple language and colorful graphics. Commentators derided it as "McPaper." Other newspapers made fun of it so much that Neuharth said, "The press is the only species besides rats that likes to eat its young." But still he pressed on. The truth is, Neuharth couldn't conceive of the possibility of failure.

With criticism flying from all sides, Neuharth faced the task of changing the very perception of his new paper.

This was his "immovable object." Could he win over enough readers and advertisers to turn *USA Today* into a financially viable, journalistically respected newspaper? Or would it be his great gamble that ultimately failed?

If anyone but Al Neuharth had been at the helm during those years, *USA Today* would have failed. But Neuharth never took no for an answer. He pushed, poked, and prodded to find ways to get to "yes." His message to us in those startup years never wavered:

> Find a way to get it done. No excuses!

Neuharth was a genius at figuring out how to create extraordinary advantages from ordinary assets. More important, his thinking was never constrained by how things had been done in the past. We've all heard the saying "Think outside the box," but it wasn't until I watched Al Neuharth up close that I truly began to understand what that meant.

From the beginning, *USA Today* was a financial black hole. Gannett poured hundreds of millions of dollars into it, an unavoidable cost for a startup that big. But Neuharth knew he needed to keep costs down as much as possible, to give the paper more time to succeed. Hiring 200 new reporters to cover the whole country would have been too expensive, so he instituted a system of "borrowing" reporters from other Gannett-owned newspapers. When *USA Today* launched, 141 out of its 218 journalists were "on loan" from other papers—on those papers' payrolls, not *USA Today*'s.

This was an audacious move, as the remaining journalists at the other Gannett newspapers had to pick up the slack. *USA Today*'s "loaner" journalists had the option of returning to their home papers if their stints didn't work out, but those who excelled at *USA Today* would eventually be offered full-time positions there. In the meantime, Neuharth planned to ride this wave of borrowed labor for as long as he could. It was a simple solution to what initially had seemed an insurmountable problem.

Neuharth also figured out creative ways to promote the paper. He was like P. T. Barnum, unafraid to employ a gimmick or two if it brought *USA Today* attention—and even details as seemingly small as the newspaper vending machines drew his attention. Until that time, they had been ugly, boxy, utilitarian contraptions. But Neuharth decided he wanted to change that. "*USA Today* is the newspaper of the future," he said, "so the vending machine should be the box of the future." The winning design looked like a television set, with rounded corners and the word *Gannett* stamped on all four sides. When you walk down the street, look for a *USA Today* box—you'll recognize the design before you have a chance to read the words on the side.

And Neuharth threw himself into marketing. When the paper was rolled out, he decided to hold launch parties in different cities at different times. This gave him nonstop promotional opportunities throughout that first year, and he really played it up. In each city he'd invite local politicians, businesspeople, advertisers, and celebrities to a huge party, which would be catered according to the local delicacy—crab dishes in Maryland, clam chowder in Boston, cheese steaks in Philly. The party would be a huge story in itself, making the local papers the next day and giving us even more exposure.

But the pièce de résistance came at the very first launch party, in Washington, D.C. Somehow, Neuharth managed to persuade President Ronald Reagan, Speaker of the House Tip O'Neill, and Senate Majority Leader Howard Baker to appear with hundreds of people on the National Mall with the Capitol as a backdrop. What were the odds of getting three of the most powerful political leaders of the land together for a joint appearance, much less one celebrating the launch of a newspaper? If you'd posed that question six months earlier, any sensible person would have said it was impossible. But achieving the impossible was a Neuharth specialty.

Of course, he'd never have been in a position to invite the president to a launch party if he hadn't stuck his neck out to start *USA Today*. But taking risks was another Neuharth specialty—and the theme of our next chapter. Read on to find out how you can manage risk and make it work for you.

CHAPTER 2

Risk

When you hear the word risk, what do you think of? Daring to make your first skydiving jump? Placing a high-stakes bet on a game or a stock tip? Telling a friend the difficult truth, even if it may change your relationship? Or pushing for a big new project or acquisition at work?

Taking a risk is both scary and exciting—scary when you focus on what can go wrong, and exciting when you consider the benefits if all goes well. The trick is to think about risk in the right way and use it to your advantage. Most people see taking risks as opening themselves up to unnecessary, maybe even dangerous, chance. But the truth is, avoiding risk won't keep you safe, nor will it guarantee a smooth ride at work or in life.

In fact, the opposite is often true. It's like the monkey parable: A monkey sees a nut in a hole, and reaches in to grab it. Once he's closed his fist around it, he can't get his hand back out of the narrow opening. Now he's stuck. He can't free himself unless he lets go of the nut, but because he's afraid to lose it, he won't let go.

Trying to avoid risk is like clinging to that nut. You may think you're playing it safe by holding on to what you have, but in reality you're just hindering your own progress.

So, how can you make risk work for you? And how can you give yourself the courage to go ahead and take risks? The answer lies in two basic rules. First:

> **Take risks that are calculated, not crazy.**

Not all risks are created equal, in work or in life. There's a big difference between rafting in whitewater with a helmet and an experienced guide and jumping on an inner-tube to soar over a waterfall on a whim. So, when you're considering taking a risk, manage the danger factor as much as you can. Ask yourself, *How can I maximize my chances of success, while minimizing my potential downside?*

About a year into my first job, at *Holiday* magazine, my boss quit. She headed the classified advertising department responsible for small ads in the back of the magazine—short, three- or four-line ads for hotels, restaurants, and summer camps. Ours was a small telephone operation with four people, separate from the group of sales guys who called on the big accounts like cars and airlines. I wasn't ready to make the jump to the big accounts, so as soon as I heard she was leaving, I wanted her job. It would be a great first step.

I made an appointment with *Holiday*'s publisher, a top executive who'd been in the magazine business for about as long as I'd been alive. "I want to talk with you about Phyllis's job," I told him. And although I had a grand total of one year of experience in advertising sales, something about my demeanor and my aggressive pursuit of the job must have convinced him I was ready.

"Okay," he said after a short interview. "We'll give you a chance. We'll also give you a three-thousand-dollar raise to reflect your new position."

Success! I was thrilled to be moving up—and yet there was already a sticking point. I knew how much money Phyllis had been making, and it was considerably more than they were offering me. I could have just thanked the publisher and taken his offer, but I decided to risk asking for more.

"I know what Phyllis was earning," I told the publisher. "And I think I ought to be paid the same salary she got, since I'll be doing the same work with the same responsibilities."

The publisher's face turned the color of a beet, as if he couldn't believe this inexperienced twenty-four-year-old would dare ask for an even bigger salary just minutes after getting her first-ever promotion. Didn't I know that moving into a higher position didn't guarantee I'd make the same salary as the person leaving?

Well, no, I didn't. But even if I *had* known, I probably would have asked for the raise anyway. The upside was obvious: making more money. The downside was . . . what? That the publisher would think less of me, or rescind the job offer? Perhaps there was a chance of that, but it was unlikely. Besides, if I didn't take the risk and ask for a higher salary, there was zero chance I would get it. As ice hockey legend Wayne Gretzky once said, "You miss 100 percent of the shots you never take."

In the end, I didn't get as much money as I had asked for, but the publisher did increase his initial offer. Nothing lost, something gained—it was the ideal outcome for taking a risk. So—think things through carefully, calculate your risks, control what you can, and take your steps accordingly. Which brings us to the second rule for making risk work for you. When assessing the downside of any risk, remember:

> **The worst-case scenario is rarely as bad as you think.**

Thousands of years ago, a handful of fortune-tellers roamed ancient China, traveling to the palaces of mandarins and predicting the future. When they were right, they were showered with riches and praised at lavish banquets. When they were wrong, they were boiled alive.

Thanks to current workplace laws, you don't have to worry about your employer boiling you alive. But you also shouldn't worry too much about other scary downsides, because the truth is, your worst-case scenario after taking a risk and failing is very rarely as bad as you imagined it to be.

I've mentioned my foray to San Francisco to work for Francis Ford Coppola's new magazine. It was risky at that point in my career to leave New York City, the epicenter of the magazine and advertising businesses, for the West Coast. It was risky to leave *Ms.* magazine, where I was gaining valuable experience and starting to make a name for myself. And it was risky to leave my friends and colleagues for something unknown, thousands of miles away. But I was ready for a change, and I fully expected the magazine to take off, and my new life in San Francisco to continue the same upward career trajectory I'd experienced in New York.

Wrong.

Within three months of moving to San Francisco, having hauled all my furniture out there and signed a year's lease on an apartment, I could already tell the magazine wasn't going to survive. We just didn't have the circulation numbers, or the advertising sales, to make a profit—nor did it look as though it would happen anytime soon. In fact, five months into it, I was so sure the magazine was collapsing that I resigned and went on a skiing vacation, rather than wait for that shoe to drop. Sure enough, while I was away, a colleague called to tell me the magazine had been shut down, with only a note posted at the entrance telling employees that the last issue had been printed, and they didn't have jobs anymore.

Talk about a worst-case scenario. My grand enterprise had just sputtered to a halt, and now there I was in California with no job and no real prospects. It would have been easy to sink into frustration. Instead, I started making calls to reestablish my contacts in New York. And as luck would have it, I was able to persuade the publisher of *Ms.* magazine, Pat Carbine, to create a position that would broaden my responsibilities beyond ad sales.

I could have chosen to focus on the "failed" aspects of my risk, but why? Ultimately, I wasn't really any worse off for my six-month experiment than if I'd stayed in New York—and in some significant ways I was better off. In fact, about eighteen months after I returned, the publisher of *New York* magazine, Joe Armstrong, asked me to join his new team as associate publisher. This was a fantastic opportunity, and within another two years I succeeded Joe as publisher.

Shortly after joining *New York,* I had a conversation with the magazine's new owner, Rupert Murdoch. At the time, Murdoch owned a handful of U.S. media properties, though now he's perhaps the world's biggest media baron, with a global media enterprise that encompasses radio, television (Fox), the Internet, and newspapers around the world. He wanted to know about my foray to California.

"Would you say that's the biggest mistake you ever made?" he asked.

"No," I told him, "I don't think it was a mistake at all." Murdoch looked at me with surprise. But I really didn't think so—not then and not now. Easy as it would have been to berate myself for pursuing a venture that ultimately failed, I still got a lot out of the experience. I'd scratched an itch to move out west and try something new, made some valuable contacts, and really enjoyed my six months in San Francisco.

So don't handicap yourself by focusing on the aspects of a gamble you took that didn't work out. Focus instead on what you learned from the things that went wrong, and how you can use that knowledge to your advantage.

This brings us to the ultimate law of risk-taking:

> **The end game is the only game in town.**

Let's say you've decided to take a risk at work—you make an unorthodox hire or propose a new way of managing a project. Anytime you shake up the status quo, you're going to face opposition. People don't like change, especially if that change involves undertaking new tasks without absolute certainty of success.

There will probably be immediate negative repercussions—say, a bumpy start for the new employee, or grumbling from colleagues who don't want to learn a new way of doing things. But stay the course, bearing in mind that the only result that matters is the *end result*. Learn to ride out the flak you receive in the interim, because attitudes will change quickly when your risk ultimately turns out well.

I learned this soon after joining *USA Today*, when I took a hard look at the advertising campaign that was promoting the newspaper to readers and realized it wasn't up to snuff. We were a young, dynamic newspaper shaking up traditional notions of journalism, yet our ads didn't communicate that at all. Even though our ad agency, Young & Rubicam, was one of the largest and most prestigious in the country, they just weren't capturing the message we wanted to get across.

One Monday, I had lunch with a guy named George Lois, a longtime New York ad man who had recently formed his own creative shop. Earlier, at the Doyle Dane Bernbach agency, he'd gained fame for a brilliant Volkswagen Beetle ad campaign, and he'd recently done great work for the fledgling MTV channel. George was about as colorful, profane, and loud as you could get without crossing the line from exuberance to insanity. My goal for the lunch was to persuade him to buy ads in *USA Today* for his clients' ad campaigns, but the conversation took quite a different turn when I asked what he thought of *USA Today*'s own advertising.

"It *sucks!*" he all but shouted, his voice booming through the restaurant. "Your product is *fantastic,* but you'd never know it from looking at those [expletive deleted] ads! *I* should be doing your campaign!"

"George, you're probably right," I said. "Our advertising isn't where it needs to be. But, as you know, there's a lot of politics involved in any ad campaign." What I was really thinking was, *George, people would think I was nuts if I suggested dumping Young & Rubicam for a little agency like yours.*

Yet the more I thought about it over the next twenty-four hours, the more I realized that not only was George Lois truly on fire to do a *USA Today* ad campaign in a way that Y&R was not, but he personally believed in the product. George saw *USA Today* as a breakthrough, unique newspaper. The Young & Rubicam execs exuded an Ivy League snobbishness toward it. I could picture them commuting in from the Connecticut suburbs, hiding *USA Today* behind the *New York Times* so no one would see them reading it—that's how little prestige the paper had in those early days, and how little respect it got. But George Lois really got what the paper was about.

So, would it really be crazy to invite him in to do a presentation? Or, as I had begun to suspect, would it be crazy *not* to? It was early enough in my tenure at *USA Today* that my colleagues were sure to look skeptically at such a radical suggestion. But if George was capable of creating a better, more exciting ad campaign, wasn't that all that mattered in the end?

I asked George to put together some prototype ads, and within two days he called to say, "Come on over and have a look." Already this was a huge difference from a major ad agency, which would have taken at least three months to do brand studies, research, focus groups, and on and on. By this time I had shared my secret project with Ray Gaulke, the president of Gannett Media Sales, who, like me, was new to the company. Ray and I were kindred souls and great pals, and we'd already found ourselves pitted together against the Gannett incumbents and "old-style" culture. He had also been president of his own ad agency and a creative director to boot, so I enlisted him to come with me to George's office, to see what he had come up with.

George's ads were fresh, exciting, and bold. His in-your-face humor really shone through, and by the end Ray and I just looked at each other with big smiles on our faces. We knew we'd found our man, and a breakthrough, sock-'em-in-the-stomach ad campaign.

But here was the tricky part. I'd done all this without mentioning any of it to my boss, Al Neuharth, so already I'd gone pretty far out on a limb. Now it was time to inch out even further. I needed to get Neuharth's okay for George to show the rest of the Gannett/*USA Today* team his work. And I needed to do it quickly, since Young & Rubicam was coming in that Friday to present their new campaign.

Have you ever wanted to suggest something new at work,

only to back down for fear people would think it was a dumb idea? Or shied away from offering an opinion or making a decision when just starting a new job because you didn't want to rock the boat? Although these are natural and understandable reactions, they also show a lack of confidence in your own instincts.

Think of it this way: If you're convinced your idea is a good one—or at least, that it has a high enough potential upside to offset the risks involved—why would you expect others to torpedo it? Believe in your own instincts, and sell your idea. If you don't, who will?

The day before the scheduled Y&R presentation, I went to Neuharth. "Al," I said, "I've invited George Lois in to show us some prototype ads. He wants our business." Neuharth looked startled. "Tell me more about this guy," he said. I explained who George was and how our invitation to him had come about, and Neuharth didn't hesitate. "We brought you in here for new ideas," he said. "So bring this guy in, and let's have a look."

The next day, Y&R presented their new campaign. And despite the agency's wealth of creative talent, you could see that nobody was excited. The ads just didn't capture the energy of this bold new newspaper. Responding to our obvious lack of enthusiasm, the Y&R people began suggesting changes—*Perhaps this headline could go with this image,* or *Maybe we could tweak the copy*—but as is usually the case, the more they fiddled, the worse things got.

When the presentation finally, mercifully, ended and the Y&R account and creative people left, I told the group that I had a surprise. "George Lois is here to make a presentation," I announced. I looked around the table, and almost every face registered confusion—who was George Lois? All I could think was, *You're about to find out.* At that moment, George came bounding in like a six-foot-three teenager hopped up on Red Bull.

George gave an Academy Award–winning performance. He

flung his jacket to the floor, tore off his tie, then flashed one prototype ad after another, prancing around the room and keeping up a running monologue sprinkled with jokes and profanity. It was epic, almost scary. I was thrilled. When he was finished, the room sat absolutely silent.

Oh God, I thought, looking around at all the dumbstruck faces. *They hated it.*

I glanced at Ray Gaulke, who raised his eyebrows ever so slightly at me. We were both thinking the same thing—how could everyone just sit there? Those ads were so damn good! My heart was pounding, and all I could think was, *We're about to get thrown right out of this room, along with sweaty, wild-eyed George Lois.*

Neuharth sat absolutely still, his expression hidden behind his dark aviator glasses. Then, mercifully, Charles Overby spoke up. A former newspaper editor, he was then working as Neuharth's executive assistant. I had always liked Charles. And although our backgrounds were very different, his being in editorial and mine in marketing, we always saw eye-to-eye about *USA Today* and most other things. Charles's sense of humor had saved many a raw moment, and I wondered how he'd break the ice now.

In his distinctive southern accent, Charles drawled, "Welllll, George, I don't know much about New York ad agencies, but those ads are the first ones I've seen that seem exactly right for *USA Today.*" On cue, as if we were watching a tennis match, all our heads swiveled to look at Al Neuharth, who paused before slowly taking off his glasses. With a smile, he said, "We've got it." Ray and I were so excited we almost danced on the conference table, and I promised myself silently that I'd follow Charles Overby off a cliff for his show of support.

We hired George for the ad promotion part of our business, a move that, predictably, was greeted with surprise and skepticism within the industry. Once again we found ourselves being questioned for an unusual decision—for taking a risk. It would have been easy to second-guess ourselves at that point, but I never doubted we'd made the right choice. And soon enough, that fact was clear to everyone.

George did such a great job that within a year we gave him all of our consumer advertising business as well, and let Y&R go completely. His ad campaign not only won awards, but changed the perception of *USA Today* practically overnight. As Charles Overby later put it, the decision to bring in George Lois was the turning point where the old Gannett faded, and the new Gannett began. He called it "breaking the egg."

The George Lois story also perfectly illustrates my favorite risk-taking secret:

> **It's easier to ask forgiveness than it is to get permission.**

When I first met George for lunch, I had no intention of hiring him for the *USA Today* account. For one thing, we weren't looking for a new ad agency, and besides, I'd never discussed the possibility with the many decision-makers that would normally be consulted for such a big, public change. So when George first suggested creating some ads, the natural response would have been to say, "Well, let me get back to you after I talk to some people."

Instead, I decided to go ahead and pursue the offer, then present it as a real alternative once I saw that George had the goods. After all, I might have been shut down if I'd asked permission to pursue it at the outset.

Don't be afraid to stick your neck out for a well-founded hunch or a well-researched idea. Unless you're working for an absolute control freak (always a possibility), your boss doesn't need or want you to go to him or her with every little decision. Take responsibility for pushing ahead with first steps; you'll save your boss time, as well as demonstrate your own confidence and savvy. And remember this valuable corollary to the "forgiveness" rule:

Know the rules, so you know which ones to break.

When I started at Hearst, I instituted an annual management conference—a chance for executives to get together and talk freely about big issues facing the company and the industry. Because we want people to feel inspired, informed, and energized, we usually hold the conferences at resort locations. We bring in a variety of speakers and encourage our executives to mix, mingle, and share ideas.

A few years ago, as we were planning the event, I wanted to turn up the voltage. I decided to bring in a speaker who would knock everybody's socks off, a man legendary for his speaking skills and personal charisma: Bill Clinton. I knew that having Clinton there would get everyone buzzing, excited about the conference and by extension excited about Hearst. He'd bring the "wow" factor, which employees would carry back to their jobs when the conference was finished.

The only trouble was, Bill Clinton did not come cheap. Because he was one of the most sought-after public speakers in the world, we'd have to be ready to spend considerably more than we usually did on speakers. I was prepared to do that. But I didn't think my boss, Victor Ganzi, would be.

So I went ahead and did it anyway, without asking Vic.

Once it was a done deal, I told him we'd gotten Clinton as a speaker for the event, and his response was what I expected.

"How much did that cost?"

"A lot," I said with a smile. "But it's worth it."

Now, Vic and I know each other very well. I have a track record with him, and we've established an essential layer of trust. I've had some bosses over the years to whom I'd never have responded in that way. But I knew the rules, I knew Vic, and, most important, I knew which rules I could break with Vic.

After that first exchange, Vic asked me a couple more times about the cost of hiring Clinton, and each time I dodged the question. The final time, he and I were on a plane together. He must have realized there was nowhere I could escape to, thirty thousand feet in the air, so as we were reviewing some monthly numbers, he looked up and said, "Cathie, you know, you never did tell me how much Bill Clinton's fee was."

I looked right at him and said, "Vic, the truth is, you will never know." And I chuckled, saying nothing more. I'm not sure he could quite believe I was refusing to tell him—I know at least one other person within earshot couldn't believe it!—but the truth was that he knew already, as Clinton's speaking fees had been reported in the press. Vic just hoped we had negotiated the fee down, which we had, sort of. But the benefits our company got from having one hundred employees rush home to tell their friends and loved ones, "I got to meet Bill Clinton!" was worth every penny we paid. The end result was a highly energized group of employees—and, as you know already, the end result is the only one that matters. Once Vic saw that I really had no intention of answering his question, he accepted it. And he never asked me again.

Rule-breaking is an underappreciated and underutilized skill. If you're like most people, you spend a lot of time and effort trying to operate within your company's or your boss's rules, even if they ultimately just get in the way. But if you look at any list of highly successful people, it's invariably populated with rule-breakers— college dropouts like Bill Gates, female trailblazers like eBay's Meg Whitman, and Internet wunderkinds like Google co-founders Sergey Brin and Larry Page, who refused to believe that a little startup couldn't take on the biggest, richest companies in cyber-space. All these people trusted their ideas, and themselves, enough to know which rules they could break. You can do the same.

NOT all of us are as naturally bold and self-confident as the trailblazers listed above, of course. And not everyone has an innate sense of what rules are okay to break. So how can you make yourself more comfortable with taking risks?

Here's one way to approach it: When we take a risk, what we're really doing is undertaking a change that, for one reason or another, can be scary. So the best way to understand risk, and use it to your advantage, is to recognize that

---

Change is the kinder, gentler side of risk.

Over the course of your life, you'll find yourself falling into certain habits. Most of them will have little impact on your pro-ductivity, success, or happiness. But others can hinder you. Learning to recognize habits that get in the way, and finding the courage to change them, will make you better off both personally and professionally. Also, if you can get accustomed to the need for periodic change, you'll be better equipped when the time comes to take bigger risks.

My first real experience managing people came at *Ms.* magazine, and it very nearly ended in a torches-and-pitchforks revolt by my staff. In those early days of the magazine, traditional big ad buyers such as cosmetics companies and automakers were reluctant to buy advertising space in a feminist magazine. Selling ads was proving much tougher than anyone had expected, and, driven by the disappointment of hearing "no" after "no" after "no," tempers often flared. That struggle, added to the fact that I was young, driven, self-assured (perhaps excessively so), and totally inexperienced in managing staff, made for a volatile combination.

In fact my direct, sometimes brusque, style grated on the staff so much, they confronted me just six months into my tenure as advertising manager. We were at an offsite sales meeting, and several of them gathered in my hotel room to demand that I resign. "Either you go or we go," they told me, threatening to quit en masse. And I could tell by looking at their faces that they weren't kidding.

What a disaster! Here we were, trying to build a magazine all about women's solidarity, and we had fractured into angry, warring factions ourselves. I knew I was perceived as bossy—in fact I knew I *was* bossy—and that people were unhappy. But I never expected they'd demand that I quit. Right away, two thoughts popped into my head. First, we had to talk our way through these problems and come up with solutions. Second, there was no way I was going to quit.

We ended up spending hours in that room, airing every conceivable grievance. You had to have a strong, assertive personality to join *Ms.* at that time, as getting such a controversial magazine started was such a huge and often discouraging task, so the women in that room were not afraid to express themselves. They really let me have it, telling me all the ways they found me deficient in my job. It was a humbling, difficult, frustrating experience.

A big part of me wanted to respond by saying, "How dare

you? Don't you see that I'm trying to do what's best for the magazine?" But another part of me realized I had to do whatever was necessary to get everyone back on the same team. Even if I believed I hadn't done anything wrong, even if I thought my staff's criticism wasn't entirely warranted, the simple truth was that we couldn't accomplish our goals in that environment of anger and mistrust. And if I wasn't leaving, and my staff refused to accept my bossy management style, there was only one option left.

I had to change.

"Listen," I told the group, "I hear what you're saying, and I'm willing to work with you to make some changes. But no way am I leaving." I looked around at their skeptical faces. "We will figure this out," I said, "because we *have* to figure it out." Eventually they agreed to give me another chance.

It wasn't easy, but the atmosphere changed. I lightened up my daily inquisition about how they were doing on accounts, we established a weekly sales meeting for updates, and although some friction remained, we all did our jobs and worked together for the next several years, getting *Ms.* off the ground. It's one of the achievements I'm most proud of in my working life—and a very good lesson, too.

What's more, I've continued since that time to be aware of my management style, refining areas that needed work over the years. I've always tended toward straightforward, unvarnished communication, which I know comes across sometimes as being uncomfortably abrupt. Though I don't take abruptness personally coming from others, I've learned over the years that many people do—so I've made a conscious effort to take the edge off.

Changing your style is one way to improve your performance at work. But don't be afraid to look outside yourself. If you're aware of ways in which your workplace can be improved, speak up! Don't be afraid to:

Blow the dust off the curtains.

When I first came to Hearst, the company had a very different reputation than it does now. Founded in 1887 when William Randolph Hearst, the mercurial son of a mining tycoon, took over the *San Francisco Examiner* from his father, Hearst today is a multibillion-dollar corporation encompassing more than 120 companies, including forty magazines in the United States and the United Kingdom, twelve newspapers, twenty-seven television stations, cable properties, and digital businesses. In the mid-1990s, when I became president of the magazine division, Hearst was firmly established as a very successful, solid, dependable, and—well, let's be honest—somewhat conservative player in the media world. People expected Hearst to be competitive, but not necessarily to lead.

Earlier in this chapter, I mentioned our annual (now biannual) management conference. By the time I invited Bill Clinton to speak, we'd been doing it for several years. But there's also a story behind the first-ever conference, which I planned my first year at Hearst.

Most management conferences are held at traditional resort areas, but for that first one I wanted to send a different message. "Let's go to the Delano Hotel in South Beach Miami," I told our PR guru, Deb Shriver. I'd never been there, but I'd read a lot about it and had heard the Delano was, shall we say, not your father's resort. Deb, who loves nothing better than to stir the pot, saw immediately what I was trying to do, and her eyes lit up with excitement.

Smack in the middle of the now-fashionable Art Deco district, the Delano Hotel is a vision in white. With its sleek furniture, polished mahogany floors, open spaces, simple elegance, and crisp white color scheme, it's a monument to cool, modern design. But the best feature of all is the profusion of sheer, billowing, white linen curtains.

The executives arrived and checked in, then gathered for a casual opening dinner on a terrace overlooking the gardens, the pool, and the ocean beyond. My decision to bring everyone to the Delano had created a buzz among the more than eighty executives. From the airy indoor-outdoor lobby to the "infinity" showers (some of the older guys thought for sure they would accidentally flood the whole room), the hotel's "barefoot chic" ethos was already challenging people's perceptions. This wasn't business as usual; everyone was being goaded into looking at things in a different way.

The next morning I opened the meeting by talking about the need to shake things up at Hearst. "We need to think in more creative ways," I told the group. "We should not be satisfied with just being a solid media player. Let's set a goal to be an innovator—a leader in our field." I talked about areas in which the company was becoming stagnant, and urged everyone to focus on ways we could inject fresh energy. Gesturing to the flowing, gauzy, floor-to-ceiling white curtains behind me, I announced, "It's time to blow the dust off the curtains at Hearst!"

If it sounds a little corny in the retelling, believe me, that metaphor for change was incredibly effective. There's something about removing yourself from the traditional setting and being in a place where the visual cues are powerful that really serves to reinforce a simple message. I wanted to shake up the parts of Hearst culture that had become staid, and the meeting at the Delano helped kick-start that process—and showed my new colleagues that I was the change agent.

Back in New York, I continued pushing that theme, not just as an abstract directive to employees, but by taking real steps to get people to understand that change was critical to our drive to succeed. To that end, I decided to take another risk.

I needed a new official photograph as Hearst Magazines president to accompany press requests, so our public relations department asked fashion photographer Patrick Demarchelier, who did a lot of work for *Harper's Bazaar*, to do the shoot. Patrick's artistic sensibility was sexy and bold—honed by years of shooting fashion magazine covers and Hollywood stars. After shooting several rather conventional angles of me standing, and then sitting in a big leather chair, he encouraged me to try something different. "Swing your legs over the side of the chair," he said.

Emboldened by his suave manner and the adventure of the photo shoot, I did. With my legs draped over the arm of the chair, half-reclining in my Ralph Lauren striped pantsuit, I thought, *This feels good.*

When the contact sheets came back, I looked through them with Deb Shriver. "I love these!" she said, pointing to the "leggy" shots. "Let's send one to the *New York Times* for their story." The *Times* was preparing a profile on me as the new president of Hearst magazines, and Deb thought these photos would perfectly illustrate the theme of shaking up the company's culture.

This was a risk. Official corporate photos usually feature a conventional pose. Would the portrait be perceived as brash and bold or, well . . . too sexy? We weren't some kind of audacious Internet startup, after all—we were a one-hundred-plus-year-old pillar of the U.S. media.

We decided to send over several different photos and let the *Times* choose which one to run. Of course, if you were a photo editor, which would you choose—the traditional shot or the leg shot? We pretty much knew which one they'd print, but I still picked up the paper with trepidation early on the morning the profile was scheduled to run. I flipped it open to the business section, and there I was—legs and all. Yikes.

What had I done? How had I let this lark from a fun photo session get all the way to the pages of the *New York Times*? I stared at the photo for a moment, then stuffed the paper in my tote bag. I jumped into a cab to head to the office, and I called Deb at home.

"I can't believe we've done this!" I told her. "What were we thinking? This is the wrong message to send—I look like I'm not serious!" Deb tried to calm me down, but I snapped my phone shut.

But gradually, over the course of the day, I began to realize we hadn't made a mistake at all. Despite my initial fears, people started calling and emailing, telling me they loved the photo and everything it implied. Sure, it was a little "out there," but wasn't that the point? As our chief marketing officer, Michael Clinton, remarked later, "If you'd come into Hearst and we were already that kind of company, it's not something you would have done. You were sending a message." And it worked. People—including our own employees—sat up and took notice. With that, we'd taken the first step toward breaking out of the stolid reputation we'd been boxed into.

IT'S all well and good for me to urge you to go out on a limb, of course—but how does that help if you're just plain scared of heights? You might have a hard time seeing beyond the possibility of failure, or be inclined simply to work around situations that require risky solutions.

The best way to get comfortable with the idea of taking risks is by breaking down how you think about them. Learn to

---

Reframe the debate.

All too often, we are the greatest obstacles to our own success. It's easy to get stuck in a mindset that prevents us from taking a fresh look at our work. No matter whether you're risk-averse, a mad daredevil, or somewhere in between, you'll benefit from learning how to *reframe the debate.*

During my first year at Hearst, I got sick of hearing "We tried that already" over and over again in response to ideas. Okay, maybe a particular idea *had* been tried before, but why not ask:

- Why didn't the idea work originally?

- Have the circumstances changed since then, in a way that might lead to success if we try it again?

- What was the fallout, and what did we learn?

As these questions show, there are plenty of ways you can learn from your earlier efforts, but instead people at Hearst had fallen into the mindset of simply repeating, "We tried that already."

"That's it," I announced one day. "I'm charging a ten-dollar fee every time that phrase comes out of someone's mouth." For a couple of months, the kitty grew. But finally everyone learned to reframe that particular debate, and it's been years since I've heard the phrase.

Now let's take that idea and expand on it. If you want to be an innovator, express yourself like an innovator. Dress in something with verve rather than a corporate uniform. Take your team offsite and do something wacky. Wear a costume to a sales meeting. Think outside the box. And recruit a few others to do the same. Pick a theme—have people dress like cartoon characters.

Similarly, if you don't want to think in clichés, don't allow yourself to speak in clichés. Practice expressing yourself in ways that will benefit you. If you deride your own work in front of others, they'll do it, too. If you're constantly self-deprecating, people will see you as uncertain of yourself. You have a lot of power to shape the public perception of yourself. Why not do it in a way that makes you look good?

Finally, why not think and act in ways that makes your product look good? Here's an example: I don't allow the use of the term *old media* at Hearst magazines. That might be the digerati's current catchall term for newspapers, magazines, books, and television, but it's not how we view ourselves, and it's not how we want others to view us. Magazines are the most highly evolved portable information sources ever invented. They're easy to carry, easy to read, don't require batteries, and don't leave ink smudges on your fingers. In fact, if you wanted to invent the perfect new medium for conveying information simply, it would look like a magazine. So why should we ever allow ourselves to be dubbed "old media"? We may not be able to stop the rest of the world from using that phrase, but we'd be foolish to use it ourselves.

So reframe the debate as you go about your work. It's the first step toward making yourself more flexible and efficient, and the ideal way to increase your own confidence—the key factor for succeeding in work and in life.

BLACK & WHITE

First Impressions

Not long ago, I was invited to speak at an event for about three hundred women executives. Just before my keynote speech, one CEO was named the winner of an award for outstanding company leadership. Everyone in the room clapped, and she began making her way to the stage.

As I watched her approach, I could hardly believe how uncertain and timid she looked. Here she was, an entrepreneur with a successful business—the reason, after all, for winning the award—and she looked like a nervous schoolgirl going to the principal's office rather than a woman being celebrated in a room full of cheering peers. Wearing a flowered print dress more appropriate for a summer picnic than a business conference, she looked down at the floor, her shoulders hunched and hands clasped in front of her. She'd obviously done great things with her company, but all I could think was *She has no idea what impression she's making right now.*

The way you present yourself makes a huge difference in how people perceive you, and not just in a superficial way. People make judgments about your abilities, self-confidence, and savvy based in part on what you choose to wear and how you carry yourself. And while you can certainly overcome negative first impressions, why create a hurdle for yourself? Why not start by making a favorable impression?

Fortunately, the four steps for making a good first impression are incredibly easy to take. Here they are, in black and white:

1. Dress for the occasion.

Dressing well is not about having the most expensive designer outfit in the room. It's about knowing what the appropriate clothes are, and wearing them with confidence. If you're interviewing at a corporate law firm, don't show up in a brightly colored minidress, no matter how good you might look in it. If you're interviewing at *Cosmopolitan* or *Harper's Bazaar,* don't show up in a dark double-breasted suit and chunky shoes. Take the time to find out what mode of dress is expected at the event, meeting, or party you're attending, because if you show up in the right thing, you'll be comfortable and more self-confident. Having your own style is fine, but if you show up in something really inappropriate, you're more likely to feel uncertain of yourself.

When I was just out of college and looking for my first job, I wangled an interview at Condé Nast, then one of the biggest magazine publishing companies in New York. I dressed in a nice, conservative suit and felt pretty good about how I looked—right up to the moment I stepped into the elevator at the Condé Nast building.

I immediately felt the penetrating gazes of half a dozen fashionably dressed young women, as they looked me up and down, several of them clutching Louis Vuitton bags. Suddenly I felt like a complete hayseed. I couldn't help but be self-conscious—exactly the opposite of how you want to feel going into an interview—

and all because I hadn't given enough thought that morning to how I should dress. That experience taught me a lesson I never forgot.

Whenever people ask me if, as president of a large magazine company, I spend a lot of time thinking about my wardrobe, my answer is a resounding *yes*. Every single morning before I get dressed, I think through the day: Who am I scheduled to see? Where are we meeting? How can I make my appearance work for me? If I have a meeting with an executive from Burberry—one of our big advertisers—you can bet I'll be wearing something from Burberry that day. Why not make a point to wear something appropriate for the occasion and person, especially when there's great potential upside and zero potential downside?

Estée Lauder, the founder of the cosmetics company that bears her name, used to make an annual appearance at the company's lavish Christmas party. One year a couple of young executives were talking a few days before the party, and one—a new hire—mentioned she hadn't thought about what to wear.

"What?!" her colleague asked, shocked. "What if you have a chance to meet Mrs. Lauder? Listen, go shopping at lunch today and buy yourself the most fabulous, most expensive dress you ever imagined buying. You have to be prepared!"

Well, this certainly got the first woman's attention, so she went out that afternoon and bought herself a beautiful, high-end designer dress. And sure enough, the night of the party, she was marched up to meet Estée Lauder herself. Mrs. Lauder shook her hand, then eyed her up and down (as only Mrs. Lauder could do), moved closer . . . and then reached up to yank the collar in back of her dress. Yes, she was checking the label. Thank goodness for the wearer, it apparently passed muster.

This is obviously an extreme example, but because the woman had entered the fashion/beauty industry, she needed to be prepared to make an investment in her wardrobe. The point is not that you should rush out and buy designer clothes. It's that you should know whom you need to make an impression on, and figure out how best to do it. That includes everything about your appearance—jewelry, shoes, hair, what bag you carry. You don't have to be a fashion plate, but you do need to show your employers and colleagues that you're attuned to your environment. And here's another hint: when in doubt, wear black. You can't go wrong with basic black.

2.　Carry yourself as though you know where you're going.

Even if you're filled with self-confidence, you'll convey the opposite if you slump around with bad posture. Here's a test: Try to picture how you'd look walking down the street in each of the following situations.

- You learn you've just lost a big contract for your company, thanks to a stupid mistake.

- You're walking to a pivotal lunch meeting with a client who's on the fence about keeping your company's services.

- You just aced an interview for a job you've always wanted.

- You just got a big raise and promotion after a glowing performance review.

When I consider each of these scenarios, I can practically feel myself sitting up straighter in my chair as I move down the list. Next time you're walking down the street, take a look at the people around you—how they walk, whether they're looking down or straight ahead, whether their shoulders are hunched. You'll find your gaze is naturally drawn to those who look comfortable and confident, as expressed in their posture. Now glance at yourself in a store window as you pass by. Do you look like someone who knows where she's going?

There are at least two benefits to carrying yourself with confidence. First, you'll make a good impression on others. Second, and no less important, you'll actually start to feel better about yourself. Several studies have found that people who consciously improve their posture actually end up improving their self-esteem. There's a real link between your physical and emotional well-being—why not take advantage of it?

There's a third benefit, too. Good posture makes you seem taller. Odd as it sounds, research has shown that being tall is an advantage in the work world. Taller men earn, on average, higher salaries and are more likely to be in positions of authority. You don't have to go out and buy twelve pairs of platform shoes, but why not maximize whatever advantages you can? Many men— even some tall ones—use discreet lifts in their shoes to give them a little more height. And women have plenty of shoe options to give them a few more inches.

3.   Look people in the eye.

When you look people straight in the eye as you're talking with them, not only do you come across as engaged and self-confident, but you more easily keep their attention, too. If your eyes dart around, or you look down at your feet or up at the ceiling, you appear hesitant and uncertain. So practice looking directly in a person's eyes during conversation, whether or not you're the one doing the talking.

That's easy enough to do one-on-one—but what about when you're in a meeting or making a presentation? Some people feel it's useful to pick a particular spot or object to look at, to combat feelings of nervousness. But it's still more effective to look people in the eye, even in a group setting. If you're making a presentation or speech, keep making eye contact with people—just do it one by one. Look around the entire room, to keep all your listeners engaged.

Learning how to make effective presentations is an invaluable skill. At Hearst, we believe it's so important that we offer everyone the chance to take a class in professional presentation. If you've never taken one, I highly recommend it. You'll learn how to communicate more effectively and present yourself in a positive fashion, skills that will benefit you in all aspects of your life—not just at work, but in your family and social life as well.

Along with making eye contact, here are a few other quick tips on greeting people:

- No limp handshakes, please. A simple, firm grasp of the hand is perfect. And if your hands tend to be sweaty, try to wipe them discreetly first.

- On the other hand, don't go too far with the firm handshake. Early in my career, in an overboard attempt to show confidence, I shook hands eagerly with a crushing grip. I stopped when one male colleague snapped, "Cathie, you don't need to break my hand!"

- No pecks on the cheek or air-kisses—save those for your friends and relatives at weddings.

4.　Express yourself clearly and confidently.

When you're speaking to someone, do you ever do any of these things?

- Insert qualifiers like "I was wondering if we might consider . . ." as opposed to simply, "Let's try . . ."

- Insert "I think" unnecessarily? I've stopped using that

phrase altogether—it only serves to water down your point.

- Downplay your own ideas with phrases like "I'm probably way off base here, but . . ." or "This might be a stupid idea, but . . ."

- Talk in circles, trying to head off objections, rather than putting your ideas out in as straightforward a way as possible?

It's easy to fall into language traps, most often when you overthink what you want to say rather than just saying it. Women in particular are prone to using such self-defeating language. Have you ever been in a meeting where a woman timidly suggests an idea, is ignored, and then a male colleague suggests the same thing ten minutes later and is hailed as a genius? It happens more often than you think—and far more often than it should.

Remember also to say what you mean, simply and directly. When I was at *Ms.* magazine, I had a great, positive meeting with a client. At the end I asked him, "So, is it possible you'll put *Ms.* on your advertising schedule?"

He leaned back in his chair, folded his hands, and regarded me with a fatherly smile. "I'm going to give you some advice, Ms. Black," he said. "Never ask someone, 'Is it possible?' After all, anything is possible. Ask instead, 'Is it probable?'"

I smiled back. "All right, then," I obliged. "Is it probable?"

"No," he said. My smile vanished—but at least he'd told me straight out, and given me a great piece of advice into the bargain.

The way you choose to speak reveals a lot about you. The more clearly you express your ideas, the more seriously they will be taken, putting you a step ahead from the get go. And don't feel the need to overexplain yourself. Have confidence that your ideas are valid on their merits.

As someone who has interviewed hundreds of people over the years, believe me, first impressions really do matter. You don't have to become someone you aren't; in fact, it would be a mistake to try to do so. But you can improve your image—and your self-image—by putting these four steps into action.

CHAPTER 3

People

When I was advertising manager at *Ms.* magazine, we worked on the tightest budget you can imagine. In the never-ending hunt for ways to save money—from renting cramped, dingy office space to hiring a bare-bones staff—we were constantly cutting corners. But one week, when I traveled to Chicago for sales calls with one of our advertising reps, a woman I'll call Bettina, I ended up cutting one corner too many.

As we checked into the hotel, Bettina—never the type to suffer in silence if she felt she was being slighted—suddenly realized I'd booked the two of us into one room.

"What is this?" she demanded. "I'm not sharing a room with you!"

"It'll be cheaper if we share one room," I said.

"No *way!*" she said. "You need to book me my own room. I am *not* doing this!"

We argued back and forth for a few minutes while the hotel

clerk waited patiently, and I finally said, "Either we share a room, or you can pay for your own. Sorry if you don't like it, but that's the way it is."

Well, that turned out to be a big mistake. That evening in the room, after we'd taken clients out for dinner, she gave me the silent treatment—except for one thing. She'd bought herself several boxes of candy, and over the course of what felt like hours, she slowly, methodically shook the contents out to nibble on. Shake, shake, shake. Crunch, crunch. Pause. Shake, shake, shake. It was torture by candy. I thought to myself, *I swear, I will never share a room on a business trip again.* And I haven't.

Bettina was right that time. No matter how much we needed to watch our budget, it didn't make sense to ask two unrelated adults to share a hotel room while on a tiring sales trip. But on many other issues, Bettina was just one of those employees who made waves seemingly for the pleasure of it. On a team filled with outspoken, type-A personalities, she was the loudest, most abrasive of them all. In her eyes, everything was a personal affront, and everyone had it in for her.

She may be an extreme example of this type, but in just about any office you'll find people like her—people who like to stir things up. How should you deal with them? What steps can you take to minimize their negative impact? And how can you head off potential conflicts between colleagues in your office?

I faced these questions head-on during my time at *Ms.* After my staff revolted, as I described in chapter 2, *Ms.* publisher Pat Carbine asked a business consultant named Margaret Henning to help us get back on track.

A dean at Simmons College who would go on to coauthor *The Managerial Woman,* Margaret had a keen sense of people. She spent time talking to each person in our department, then invited me to meet with her to discuss what she'd learned and how we might move forward. We went to a nearby diner, and as I settled into my chair, Margaret got right down to business. "So, Bettina is a bitch," she said, leaning forward and looking me straight in the eye. "What are you going to do about it?"

I looked at Margaret in astonishment. I had been so close to our difficult staff situation that I no longer had any perspective—I'd assumed the problem must really be with me. But suddenly I realized that Margaret had nailed it perfectly: Bettina *was* a bitch. Yet what could I do about it? Bettina was who she was, and I certainly couldn't change her. That's when I learned the first great rule of managing people:

> **Different folks require different strokes.**

The first year that I managed my team at *Ms.*, I made the mistake of dealing with everyone the way I'd want to be dealt with myself. I didn't waste time with a lot of aimless pleasantries, but got directly to the point. I told them exactly what was on my mind when I felt they needed to know it and discouraged a lot of back-and-forth when someone disagreed with my opinion. I was businesslike—some might say blunt.

Because this was how I liked to be managed, I assumed this approach was best for everyone. But it didn't take into account the simple fact that people are different and respond to situations differently. At first I was frustrated that people responded to my management style in ways I didn't understand. I wanted them to adjust, since I believed my way made the most sense. After a while, though, I finally figured out that it was easier—and more effective—for me to make small adjustments than to try to get everyone else to change for me. After all, the end game was not to impose my way of doing things on everyone; it was to draw out others' best work performances. Once I began focusing on that, the clashes eased off.

Even now, many years and many jobs later, I still keep that rule in mind. As the president of a magazine company, I'm a business-and-marketing mind dealing with creative minds. If I tried to deal with the editors of our magazines in the same way that I do our marketing and financial executives, they'd look at me as if I were speaking French. Instead, I take pains to talk about what interests them the most: cover choices, their favorite article in an issue, whether they're working on any books, the website traffic, and on and on. Of course we talk about the current stats of the magazine, such as newsstand sales and subscription response, or how much a photo shoot costs and whether they're staying on budget. But it can't just be business metrics.

Valerie Salembier, the publisher of *Harper's Bazaar*, had a similar revelation at the end of her tenure as associate publisher at *USA Today*. She often worked late into the evening, and in the days before email became commonplace, she'd go around to her associates' workstations before heading home, posting little yellow sticky notes on their computer screens. Those notes became a running joke around the office—people started calling them "yellow meanies" because they dreaded coming to the office in the morning to find a half-dozen of them, with terse comments or instructions (and occasional profanity), stuck on their computer screens.

At Valerie's farewell party when she left *USA Today* to become publisher of *TV Guide*, her colleagues had the last laugh. We were all gathered at the "21" Club in midtown Manhattan, and as drinks flowed and good cheer prevailed, Valerie's team presented her with a big board covered with her yellow meanies. The recipients proceeded to read each of their favorites aloud as everyone howled, and the legend of the yellow meanies was cemented forever in *USA Today* lore. But as Valerie told me later, she realized then that her sticky notes meant different things to different people—and that even though people were making light of them that night, some had found them aggressive or even offensive. Today she's best known for going the extra mile for her staff and clients, such as making homemade Italian meals for new hires, or giving small gifts to compliment an effort on a big sale.

The truth is, some degree of friction is inevitable in any workplace, especially one populated with ambitious, smart, aggressive people. Friction can be useful, boosting the energy in the office and stoking competition. In fact, it often helps to have flamethrowers and others who don't quite fit in, as they bring a new dynamic to the office. So if you find yourself working on a team with someone like that, just stay focused on the end game. The reality is, if you're producing the results that your job requires you to produce, whatever happens in the interim—no matter how intense or frustrating it may seem at the time—is just noise.

The same applies if you find yourself supervising a flamethrower. When one person constantly creates friction with the rest of the team, ask yourself whether that person is ultimately contributing to—or even increasing—the overall productivity. If so, he or she is worth keeping around. It's only when that balance shifts that you need to figure out the next step. In the case of *Ms.* magazine, we did keep Bettina around, and despite the very real friction she created in the office, she played a big role in helping get the magazine off the ground. And that, ultimately, was what mattered.

No matter what your relationship is with your team members, you'll always get better results from them if they know you're on their side. You don't have to create an us-versus-them mentality, pitting your team against the rest of your organization or company, but—

Fight for your people.

One morning during the time Valerie Salembier and I were both at *USA Today,* I walked into my office to find an envelope on my chair. The end-of-year bonuses had just been distributed, and she'd left hers for me to see, with a note saying she was upset. Valerie had worked incredibly hard over the previous year, traveling every week (often more than once), taking on huge responsibilities, and producing amazing results. When her bonus check had arrived, she'd torn it open with high hopes, only to feel let down—was this how much the company valued all her effort? It seemed to Valerie no better than a token bonus.

There's nothing worse than feeling unappreciated in your job. In Valerie's case, her disappointment wasn't just about the size of her bonus, but about feeling like her extra effort had been accepted as just a matter of course. What was the point of killing herself in her job if her bosses—including me—were indifferent to all her effort?

I took her check and note in to CEO Al Neuharth and told him I thought Valerie deserved more than what she'd received. He looked at her check, then reminded me that *USA Today* followed a preset formula for bonuses and that Valerie had received the highest possible bonus under the system. It was unfortunate that she wasn't happy with it, but those were the rules, and they applied not just to Valerie but to everyone in the company.

At that point I had a choice. I could go back to Valerie, re-explain the bonus system, and urge her to accept it, or I could continue to fight for her to receive more compensation. Did it make sense to bend the rules for one person? Would everyone in the company start demanding bigger bonuses if and when word got out that one person had gotten one? There was certainly a risk of that—but it was outweighed, I thought, by the fact that Valerie had gone so far above and beyond the call of duty.

"I still think Valerie deserves something extra," I told Neuharth. "She worked like a dog, made huge gains, and deserves to know the company appreciates it."

He thought for a moment, then said, "Okay, let's give her two first-class air tickets to anywhere she wants. She can take a nice vacation somewhere."

When Valerie heard the news, she was thrilled. Of course, her two first-class tickets probably didn't cost the company more than about $5,000 back then—a nice amount, but not earth-shattering for a person at her level. But she was so pleased at having her work recognized that the gift buoyed her well into the next year. And it solidified her knowledge that I would stand up for her, which may have been more important than anything.

Just as managers need to stand up for their employees, the reverse is true, too. Even though your boss is a level above you, she still needs your support in the office. The higher up the ladder a person gets, the less likely she is to receive thanks or words of support. And while it's true that people in positions of power don't typically require a lot of hand-holding, I can tell you from experience that a well-timed note of thanks, or a word of praise in front of others (as long as it's offered sincerely, and not as a way to score points), is always welcome.

A little earlier in this chapter, I mentioned Pat Carbine, the publisher of *Ms.* Along with the more high-profile editor, Gloria Steinem, Pat was the driving force behind getting *Ms.* off the ground. More important for me, personally, she was a confidante and adviser during a critical period in my career. At the time, I didn't think of myself as someone who wanted or needed mentoring. But looking back, I now believe that it can only help you to

Find yourself a mentor.

I first met Pat when she interviewed me for the advertising manager position at *Ms.* as the magazine was about to launch. I'd been working at *New York* magazine, and though I was certainly enjoying my job, I was excited at the idea of joining this ground-breaking feminist magazine. So when I went for my first interview with Pat, I dressed for success, put on my most winning smile, and aimed to charm her right into a job offer.

Well, Pat wasn't convinced. She liked me right away, I could tell, but no job offer came. A week or so later we had another interview, and again I expected an offer. Again, I was disappointed. This went on for several more weeks, until I came home after the fifth interview or so and my then-husband, Jim O'Callaghan, said, "Cathie, hasn't she offered you a job *yet*?"

As I would soon learn, Pat Carbine was—and still is—a very deliberate, patient person. She knew the road ahead would be a tough one, and she wanted to make absolutely sure she was building the right team. As she later told me, she wanted to make sure she hired "people I'd want in the trenches with me when the shooting started." So the interview process went on until Pat was finally convinced that, despite my youth and inexperience managing people, I was the right person for the job.

Once that had happened, Pat worked hard to bring out the talents she thought she saw in me. And I discovered that I could learn not only from her guidance, but simply by watching her work. Pat had a way of managing people with easygoing good humor, and she knew how to pull great performances out of them without any brow-beating. She hated confrontation—she'd take a plane, train, or bus to get away from it—but she made her style work for her, and I learned a lot from it.

Pat also gave me excellent advice, sometimes when I didn't want to hear it—such as the time she saved me from making a big career mistake out of my own impatience. It was hard to do, but I needed to make a leap of faith to

---

Trust the voice of experience.

By the time I'd been at *Ms.* for a couple of years, I'd moved quickly up the career ladder, and I was eager to keep rising. My goal, which I'd made no attempt to hide, was to become publisher of a magazine. In the magazine world, the editor-in-chief is the top-ranking employee on the editorial side, the person responsible for the stories, photos, and illustrations that go into the magazine. The publisher is the top-ranking employee on the business side, responsible for ensuring that the magazine sells enough copies and brings in enough advertising dollars to succeed as a business. For an advertising person like me, rising to the rank of publisher would amount to becoming captain of my own ship.

So, at age thirty, when I was offered the chance to become publisher of a small magazine called *Connecticut,* I was ready to jump. This was the opportunity I'd been waiting for, and it was about to become a reality. I couldn't wait to tell Pat the news.

What I didn't expect was Pat's lukewarm response. "Whoa, slow down there," she said. "Are you sure this is what you want to do?"

"Of course it is," I said, feeling a little stung by her words. "You know being a publisher is exactly what I've been wanting to do— and now I have the chance. Are you saying I shouldn't take it?"

"Cathie," she said, "do you really want to be publisher of a small magazine based in a little Connecticut town two hours away from New York City? I know you're excited, but it would be a mistake to jump at the first opportunity. You need to wait for the *right* opportunity."

I tried to argue that bigger and better job offers would come more quickly if I went ahead and took this one, but Pat was adamant. "Don't do this, Cathie," she said. "It's not the right place for you. Be patient. I promise, you will be a publisher in time."

I was in a quandary. I wanted so badly to be a publisher, and I'd been really excited to get this offer. I knew and liked the owner of *Connecticut* magazine, who had personally asked me to come on board. I was truly torn, but in the end I decided to listen to Pat. And she was right. Though I wondered at first whether I'd made a mistake in taking her advice, within two years I was made associate publisher of *Ms.* And three years after that, I returned to *New York* magazine as publisher.

Would my career truly have suffered if I'd ignored Pat's advice? Even if I'd gone to Connecticut, I would probably have advanced to bigger magazines. Yet choosing to stay put ensured that I maintained my growing profile in the New York magazine world, a step that ended up paying off sooner rather than later. With her outside perspective and experience, Pat was able to see clearly how my career trajectory might spike if I displayed a little more patience. I'm grateful she suggested it, and glad I was able to set aside ambition long enough to take her advice.

What kinds of issues are you facing in your work life right now? Do you ever ask yourself these questions:

- What is the smartest next step for building my career?

- Are my skills actually better suited to a different kind of work from what I do now?

- Should I take a break in my career and get an MBA?

- How can I use my contacts to create new opportunities for myself?

If you're like most people, you think about one or more of these questions nearly all the time. Let's face it, figuring out how to navigate the world of work isn't easy. If you're smart and driven, you can certainly do it on your own—but why would you, if you can get the benefits of someone else's experience and wisdom? Don't be afraid to ask for help. Seek out a mentor—someone who knows you, someone you can trust, talk with, and ask advice of. And don't think you have to limit yourself to just one mentor, either. Over time, your needs will change, and there will be others who can help you in the new phases of your career.

On the flip side, unless you're in your very first job, you've already accumulated enough experience to help someone else. Use your experience to

> **Be a mentor, too.**

Now, before we get any deeper into this topic, I should clarify what I mean by mentoring. The truth is, I've never really liked that word. It sounds overly structured, not to mention boring. If you mentor someone, it doesn't mean you have to become their big brother or sister. You don't have to dispense dime-store wisdom and track every move they make. What I'm talking about is simpler and more organic than that; it's seeing potential in someone, and doing what you can, when you can, to help him or her reach that potential. At the most basic level, it's letting the person know you're there to help.

In any office, you'll usually find at least one young person with that something extra, a special spark. There are plenty of good people around, but when one in particular pops out of the soil like a little asparagus, that's the kind of person you ought to get to know—the future leader, creative type, or idea person. For one thing, helping to grow their skills will help your company. For another, you'll develop a strong relationship with a talented person, and that can certainly come in handy as you both continue to move up in the working world.

Ask successful men or women about their early years in business, and nearly every one will be able to tell you about the first person who showed faith in his or her abilities or offered genuine encouragement. In many cases they've stayed close to each other over the years and the relationship has continued to benefit them both.

That's true in my case, too. Pat Carbine and I have stayed very close, and over the years we've helped each other numerous times. In 2006, when I was fortunate enough to receive the Henry Johnson Fisher award for lifetime achievement in magazines, I could have chosen a media celebrity to introduce me, but I asked Pat to do it. She gave a beautiful speech, and as I sat with my family in a ballroom filled with industry colleagues, I felt incredibly moved hearing her describe the work we'd done together in helping to change the perception of women in business. It was a moment I'll never forget.

So remember that the benefits of mentoring go both ways. Seek out talented people both above and below you on the career ladder; over the years these relationships will pay off handsomely, and they might even lead to deep and enduring friendships.

A COUPLE of years ago, a Hearst executive walked into my office with a complaint.

"Cathie," she said, "I just heard there's a meeting this afternoon that I should be in on, and nobody told me about it. I don't know why I'm being shut out, but I should definitely have been included."

"So go to the meeting," I told her. "Assume it was an oversight, and go take your rightful place." She looked surprised, but later in the day she did just that. And as it turned out, she hadn't been intentionally excluded—it was an honest mistake. She'd made a mistake, too, in forgetting this important rule:

Don't personalize things that aren't personal.

Offices are kind of like families—you're thrust into close relationships with people you'd normally have nothing to do with. And just as in families, this provides all kinds of opportunities for conflict, whether real or imagined. Yet, in my experience, I've found there's actually less real personality conflict than people imagine. All too often, someone takes a stray comment or missed connection as a personal affront when it wasn't intended that way. And, unfortunately, once a degree of friction or mistrust has been established between people, it often becomes a self-fulfilling prophecy, and problems really do start to develop.

How do you respond when

- a group of people in the office goes out for lunch to discuss an upcoming project and you're not invited?

- someone interrupts you at a meeting to shoot down your idea?

- a colleague responds to your email with a sharp critique, cc-ing others in your department?

For many people, the natural response in such situations is to feel both professionally affronted and personally slighted. Sometimes we're so attached to our own ideas that we can't imagine people have real objections to them, so we assume it must be a personality thing. And in certain cases it is, of course. But here's a little secret: no matter whether a conflict represents a legitimate criticism, a personality clash, or something in between, you should always treat it as if there were no personal component at all.

Making the choice to view conflict in the office as professional rather than personal accomplishes two key things. First, it ensures that you don't accidentally overreact and see a personal component where there is none. Second, it effectively defuses any personality conflict that might really exist. Think of it this way: someone in the office who tries to provoke you personally is really trying to establish dominance or control over you. By choosing not to respond on that level, you deny him or her that control. There's very little upside to engaging with a colleague in a personal war—but there's a huge upside in refusing to let someone drag you into one.

I once had a colleague who made a habit of showing me up in meetings. Because we worked on the same team, we shared information in advance—yet always, when it came time to meet with others in the company, he'd whip out some new fact or piece of data that would make me look unprepared. It drove me *crazy*. I couldn't figure out why he felt compelled to undercut me constantly. And when I asked him about it, he claimed not to know what I was talking about.

Here was a conflagration in the making. Over time I got more and more irritated, and my agitation began affecting our working relationship. Then one afternoon I had an epiphany: this guy was a favorite in the department, he wasn't going anywhere, and I was going to have to deal with him for a long time to come. I couldn't change him, so I needed to find a way to work effectively with him.

I set a goal of letting go of the feelings of irritation that were impeding our working relationship. If his little jabs in meetings were the worst I could expect from him, I could live with that. It was time to focus on the good things about my colleague, of which there were plenty. In addition, I set up regular meetings just for the two of us so he had a chance to air concerns and differences of opinion on strategy, in private.

From that moment on, it was surprisingly easy to let go of the negative emotion that had been building. My colleague continued occasionally to trot out his new facts at meetings, but I learned to work around his habit. Our relationship improved dramatically, and we enjoyed many more years of productivity while on the same team.

This technique works great for small irritations. But what if the clash we're talking about is more than just an angry word or two? How can you deal with someone who has behaved totally inappropriately toward you? I'd love to give you permission to let the air out of their tires or embarrass them at the office holiday party, but although the short-term gratification might be immense, the only road to take is the high road. It's best in the long run to

---

Make your life a grudge-free zone.

One afternoon while I was at *Ms.,* I paid a visit to the media director of a New York–based ad agency. I'd set up the meeting to present to him our brand-new subscriber survey, a comprehensive snapshot of who was buying and reading *Ms.* magazine.

Lots of magazines undertake subscriber surveys as a routine part of their ad sales strategy, but in the case of *Ms.* this was a critical step. The women's movement was in full swing, and so was the controversy over what it all meant. News coverage mostly focused on the movement's more radical elements—the TV clips were all about bra-burnings, demonstrations, and fist-shaking women—which frightened off many potential ad buyers for *Ms.* We needed to get the message out that our magazine had a desirable reader base for advertisers, and our subscriber survey was the way to do it.

My appointment with this media director was scheduled for 2:00 p.m., the worst time of day for a meeting. For one thing, people's metabolisms slow as they digest lunch, and they're often sleepy or unfocused. For another, at that time the three-martini lunch was still in vogue. Very soon after arriving for my appointment, I realized that the media director was enjoying the effects of just that kind of lunch.

Still, I was primed for the meeting, excited about our subscriber survey, and ready to make my pitch, so I forged ahead. I handed him the survey—printed on shocking-pink paper, with the word *Ms.* in big white letters on the front—and launched into my spiel, turning over page after page.

From the start, I could tell he wasn't really paying attention. Slumped back in his chair, wearily rubbing his eyes, he looked incredibly bored. But I soldiered on, hoping I could get him engaged if I just pumped up the energy a little. Then, just as I was getting into the heart of the presentation, I saw him pick up his survey off the table and slowly raise it toward his face. To my shock, he let loose with the loudest, most theatrical, most prolonged *hhhhaaawwwccckk* sound I'd ever heard. Suddenly it was as if we were a couple of ten-year-olds on the playground; I watched in horror as he prepared to hurl the biggest gob of spit in history onto my survey.

He didn't actually spit, thank goodness. But in case his message wasn't already clear enough, he turned and tossed the survey to the floor. I looked at him in amazement, the blood rushing to my face. I could hear my heart beating in my ears, I was so furious. I turned to the only other person in the room, a junior account guy from their office, who sat quietly, looking at the floor, afraid to intervene.

"This meeting is over," I snapped. I stood up, grabbed my things, and stormed out of that room as fast as my legs would take me.

In my entire life, I'd never been so insulted. I fumed all the way back to *Ms.* and rushed straight into Pat Carbine's office. My face was red, my eyes were moist with tears I was barely holding in, and I was shaking. I told Pat what had happened, and she immediately placed a call to the president of the ad agency, told him the story, and demanded an apology.

"What time was the meeting?" the president asked Pat.

"Two o'clock," she replied. "What difference does it make?"

"Oh," he said with a chuckle. "Well, he'd probably had a few drinks at lunch. You should try to make appointments with him in the morning if you can."

If ever there was a time when I had a right to hold a grudge, this was it. This guy had tried to humiliate me on so many levels—as a businessperson, as a guest in his office, and as a woman—that I couldn't imagine dealing with him ever again. I'd been upset with people in the workplace before, but nothing compared with the level of anger and disgust I was feeling now.

As usual, Pat Carbine was my guiding voice of reason. With her steady, deliberate, unruffled personality, she was the perfect person to make me understand that holding a grudge against this man would not help me in the least. In fact it would probably hurt me, since he was a media director at an ad agency, and we were likely to cross paths again. Even if he was completely at fault, I'd only make things harder on myself by refusing to let go of the incident.

Sure enough, I did find myself dealing with this guy again. He eventually moved out west to work for an automotive company, and I ended up meeting with him a number of years after the spitting incident. When we sat down in a conference room together, he looked at me with a half-smirk and said, "Do you remember that time we met in New York?"

"Oh," I said, a big smile on my face, "you don't really think I could have forgotten that, do you?" This threw him off balance for a moment, until he realized from my demeanor that I had no intention of making an issue out of it. With that out of the way, we got down to business, and we were able to deal with each other professionally and efficiently.

So do yourself a favor. No matter how tempting it is, no matter how natural it feels, don't give in to a grudge. Remember that the only person it will hurt, in the end, is you.

ONE afternoon at *New York* magazine, I found myself irritated with the promotion manager. Something she'd done—I don't even remember now what it was—just set me off, and I went tearing into her office.

I stood in front of her desk for a moment, snapping at her, before realizing there was someone else in the office with us, sitting behind me on the couch. I turned to find her husband sitting there, a look of shock on his face. And all of a sudden I felt incredibly embarrassed. I must have looked like a lunatic, racing in and using that tone with her, something I'd never have done had I known he was there. I took a deep breath, apologized, and walked out of the office.

Over the next few days I thought about my reaction. If I was embarrassed to be caught speaking like that in front of someone, then why was it okay to do it when no one else was around? Wasn't it better to deal with people in ways I didn't need to hide? Or, more important, in ways I wanted to be dealt with myself?

Besides that, what had I really expected to gain? Sure, it felt good to let off some steam, but just like the pleasure of giving in to a grudge, this, too, was a fool's errand. My ultimate goal was not, after all, to make her feel bad or regretful. It wouldn't have helped the team at all if she had taken my criticism personally, which she was more likely to do considering how I delivered it. The ultimate goal, of course, was to improve her performance, so she wouldn't make such mistakes again. And the more I thought about it, the more I realized there were two ways to help do that:

> **Be generous with praise, and careful with criticism.**

At its most basic level, business isn't really about numbers, markets, and products. It's about people. The better you understand people—your customers, your bosses, your colleagues—the more successful you'll be. And one big key to understanding people is to realize that they aren't as complicated as you might think.

People like to be praised, and they don't like to be criticized. Pretty simple, right? Praise makes us feel energized and capable, and criticism makes us feel bad and uncertain. So, logically, you should praise your colleagues freely, but confine your criticisms to those things that are truly important. Remember that words matter, as does the way you deliver them.

During the late 1990s, *Redbook* magazine hosted a big luncheon with First Lady Hillary Clinton at the White House. Kate White, *Redbook*'s editor at the time, was hosting the luncheon, and she was nervous. She'd met numerous celebrities in the course of her career, and she knew her way around a star-studded event. But being at the White House was different. In the moments leading up to the luncheon, as all the last details were attended to, Kate found her mind racing: *Is my dress too short? Did we remember everything? Am I going to screw up my introduction?* She was as nervous as I've ever seen her, before or since.

As we walked together up the magnificent staircase leading to the very elegant East Room, I leaned close and whispered, "Kate, you look so good in that dress." And as she told me later, that small vote of confidence snapped her back out of her anxious swirl. She'd wanted to look great, so she'd worn a short dress and a pretty scarf—but once she was in the White House, with those majestic rooms and sweeping porticoes, she'd felt awkward—maybe she should have worn something more sedate. Hearing me compliment her dress restored her confidence, and as she strode to the podium to speak, you'd never have thought she'd had a moment of doubt.

Words carry a huge amount of weight, so choose and use them carefully. Equally important, always keep in mind the person to whom you're delivering your message. If you take the time to consider how to connect most effectively with that particular person, you'll accomplish much more—as this next story will show.

Make Your Moment Count:
O, the Oprah Magazine

In late January 1999, I traveled back to my hometown of Chicago for a meeting. But not just any meeting. I'd come with Ellen Levine, then the editor-in-chief of Hearst's *Good Housekeeping* magazine, to make a presentation at Oprah Winfrey's production company, Harpo, Inc. We wanted to pitch Oprah on the idea of doing her own magazine.

Oprah was already hugely successful by then, with a top-rated television show, an Oscar nomination for her starring role in *The Color Purple,* and numerous Emmy awards to her name. Her message of optimism and self-acceptance had proven an inspiration for tens of millions of women, her book club was having an unprecedented impact on the publishing world, and she'd moved steadily up the "most influential people" lists. But although we were thrilled to get in the door at

Harpo, Oprah had made it clear she was far from sold on the idea of doing a magazine.

"You know," she'd told Ellen, "lots of people have brought this up to me, and I'm not really interested in doing a magazine. But come on out to Chicago and we'll talk."

We were scheduled to meet with Oprah's lawyer/agent Jeff Jacobs, and we didn't know whether Oprah herself would come. I'd never met Oprah, but I was convinced her clear, uplifting message and personal charisma would make her a natural for a magazine. Oprah was understandably protective of her name and image, so we needed to reassure her on two points: first, that a magazine would be a positive vehicle for her message, and, second, that Hearst was the right partner for her in such a venture. We knew other magazine companies were approaching Oprah, too—as she later said, five different executives had called her in a six-month period—so this pitch was our big chance to win her over.

Ellen and I were shown into a small, tastefully decorated conference room and seated at a long table. Jeff Jacobs came in with a couple of people from Harpo's public relations team, and we started the meeting. We hadn't gotten much beyond opening pleasantries when the door to the conference room suddenly swung open, and Oprah breezed in.

I've met a lot of powerful, charismatic people over the years, from politicians to CEOs to movie stars—it comes with the job. But I honestly have never in my life met anyone who transforms a room like Oprah Winfrey.

She's like a 10,000-watt bulb, an electrifying presence. She looked just like she does on TV—with the familiar sweep of hair, expressive eyes, and ready smile—yet somehow it felt completely different seeing her in person. I know it sounds strange, but the aura Oprah brings into a room is just dazzling. For a brief second after she walked in, I was speechless. Then I stuck out my hand to greet her.

This was the moment we'd been waiting for. I truly believed we could create a fantastic, groundbreaking magazine with Oprah, and now here we were, face to face, with our one chance to convince her. Were we ready? It was time to

---

Seize the moment.

Let's put that meeting on freeze-frame for just a second. What do I mean by "seize the moment"? It might not be what you're thinking, so let me explain.

We knew we'd have just this one shot with Oprah, so that morning Ellen and I had taken extra care to make sure we were completely ready. We woke up early and went over our materials together. We dressed to impress, made sure we got to Harpo's offices fifteen minutes early, and were both pumped and ready to go. When Oprah walked in, my adrenaline kicked in and I was "on"—ready to give the most energetic, dynamic presentation I could.

Yet none of this would have mattered if we hadn't begun seizing our moment weeks before the actual moment came. As soon as we learned we'd get a meeting at Harpo, Ellen, Deb Shriver, and I sprang into action to prepare the most complete and compelling presentation we possibly could. We did meticulous research to lay the groundwork for our presentation to shine. It's like building a spectacular new home—no matter how beautiful or stylish the architecture may be, a house is worth nothing if it lacks the plain old unglamorous foundation that takes so much spadework to create.

Weeks before the meeting, we started gathering materials for our presentation. We wanted Oprah to really sense the possibilities of the magazine, so Ellen and a small editorial and art team created pages for her to touch and feel. Ellen put together mock covers, with several logos in different typefaces, to show Oprah what her magazine might look like. We ordered a variety of high-quality paper samples, so she could feel the gloss for herself and see which ones she liked. We bound some of those blank pages together, to give her a feel of the weight and heft of her magazine. And we even created mock tables of contents, to show the range of what her magazine could cover month after month.

Two nights before our meeting in Chicago, Deb, Ellen, and I sat in a conference room at Hearst, preparing our presentation packets. As we sat together stuffing papers into portfolio folders, I suddenly felt transported back to *Ms.* magazine, to the days when our whole advertising team would work together, stuffing envelopes and getting ready for sales trips. It had been years since I'd done anything like this, and I was loving every minute of it. The three of us talked and laughed as we worked, and our excitement grew about the upcoming meeting.

The next day, a Wednesday, Ellen and I flew to Chicago. We wanted to get there a day early, so we wouldn't risk being late if something went wrong with our flights. That night in my hotel room, I lay awake thinking about the next morning's meeting. We'd done everything we could to prepare, and as I went over our presentation in my mind, I felt confident that we'd also followed the second rule of seizing your moment:

Tailor your message to your audience.

When Oprah walked into that room, she was as focused and open to our message as she would ever be. So the first thing we did was speak to her in a language she knew better than any of us.

"We'd like to show you a video," I said, and asked for the lights to be dimmed. On a large television screen at the front of the room, the video launched with a woman's voice-over saying, "She's down to earth! I mean, I can kind of relate to her." For the next four minutes, we all watched as the video cut between clips of women randomly interviewed at a Virginia shopping mall, urging Oprah to do a magazine ("You go, girl!"), and Ellen Levine explaining how and why it would work. "TV whets your appetite," Ellen said at one point, "and magazines fill your stomach."

It wasn't expensive or slickly produced, but the video was definitely compelling. When I glanced at Oprah, she was completely absorbed in it, watching intently yet with a slight smile on her face. Here were the everyday women she reached through her television show, and they were practically begging her to do a magazine. The excitement of the women on screen was palpable, and as I watched the video in that darkened room, I felt it, too.

The lights went back up, and Ellen and I immediately handed out our packets of materials—the cover mock-ups, tables of contents, glossy paper samples, and bound prototype magazines. Oprah is not only a very visual person, but a very tactile one, so we'd wanted her to have something to touch and feel. She smiled as she flipped slowly through the pages, but we weren't there yet.

As Oprah said later in a speech at the annual American Magazine Conference, "They had this fabulous presentation. It was just dazzling . . . But I said, 'No, you know, I just feel that I have a lot of responsibilities, I've done thousands of shows, I see no reason why I should get involved in the magazine business. I really don't even know anything about it except I've bought magazines myself over the years.'"

And this was the crux of the matter: What was the upside for Oprah—already so busy taping two shows daily—in doing a magazine? For most people the upside would be things like increased personal visibility, the potential for big profit, and the chance to expand a brand. But anyone who'd followed Oprah's career knew these weren't the things that motivated her. Oprah had become successful not because she sought success, but because she offered an authentic, sincere message that audiences wholeheartedly embraced—to "live your best life." She was about connection, and she would only want to do a magazine if she believed it would offer an effective additional channel for getting that message out.

"You want to know why you should do a magazine?" Ellen said. "Because you love the written word. And a magazine is the written word. It is tangible, you can pass it on, it stays with you." Oprah nodded and continued to flip through the pages.

With her hugely successful book club, Oprah was of course no stranger to the power of the printed word. She loves to read, and has spoken movingly about how books and magazines offered her a respite from her difficult childhood. Ellen continued, "You go on the air every day, you say what you say, and no doubt you say a lot of good things. But then it's gone. It's out there. Who knows where it is? But the written word—you can hold it in your hand. You can come back to it."

Now, if you subscribe to the idea of business being all about numbers, this pitch might seem pretty foolish. Yet the beauty of pitching Oprah Winfrey on her own terms—with message rather than money, and with personal impact rather than profit—was that it was also a sound business strategy. In my experience, you can't start or grow a successful magazine if you focus solely on the numbers, advertising, circulation, or any other metric. First and foremost, you have to offer a compelling and differentiated product to readers. The rest will follow. Oprah's authenticity had already proven to be incredibly compelling, so it didn't make sense to focus on the metrics, as those weren't what motivated Oprah anyway.

In fact, during the whole ninety-minute meeting, we didn't discuss specific metrics at all. We talked about what the magazine might look like, what it could be called (*Spirit* was one of our early suggestions, though we always hoped that Oprah would put her name on it), and whom it would serve. The feeling in the room started to shift; in fact, it started to feel like the atmosphere of Oprah's show—positive, warm, and optimistic.

Fortunately we had a head start with Oprah in terms of winning her trust. Over the years, she'd been on the cover of *Good Housekeeping* several times (those issues were always best-sellers), and she appreciated the fact that we'd always been straightforward in our stories and our dealings with her. Our writers had never tried to trick her into revealing something juicy or embarrassing, and she liked the cover photos our editors had chosen. In fact she once told Ellen that a *Good Housekeeping* photo of her and her two dogs was her favorite cover ever. So, thanks in large part to Ellen, we had an established level of trust to build on.

At one point Oprah said, "You know, a couple of

days ago, a woman in the audience stood up after the show and said, 'You should do a magazine!'" Someone in our meeting made a crack about whether Hearst had planted that person (we didn't!), but by now it appeared clear that, for Oprah, many factors seemed to be coming together. She operates very much on gut instinct, and, fortunately for us, we'd tapped in to something.

As we wrapped our presentation, Oprah prepared to go. She told us she hadn't made up her mind yet about whether to do a magazine and said she wanted to pray about it. But then she added in that velvet voice, "If I do one, I'll do it with Hearst." With that, she left the room.

Ellen and I managed to pack up our things, shake hands with Jeff Jacobs and the Harpo public relations team, and get all the way down to our waiting car before erupting like a couple of shrieking teenagers. In the backseat of the car, we high-fived like we'd just won the Super Bowl, laughing and then fumbling for a phone so we could call Deb Shriver. She answered on the first half-ring. "So how'd it go?" she got out, before our delighted whoops told the story.

Launched in April 2000, *O, the Oprah Magazine* quickly became the most successful magazine startup in history. While most magazines take at least five years to become profitable, *O* turned a profit from its very first issue. *Adweek* named *O* the Startup of the Year, and *Advertising Age* named it Best Magazine of the Year and Best Launch of the Year. It has continued to win numerous magazine awards through the years, and it is

Hearst's second-most-profitable magazine—even though we split the profits with Oprah fifty-fifty.

Under the guidance of Oprah, editor-in-chief Amy Gross, and editor-at-large Gayle King, *O* is a consistently superior editorial product. During its seven years in existence, it has succeeded in reaching a constituency that was craving the positive message it delivers, and has expanded Oprah's message in just the way we hoped and expected.

Yet it pays to remember that we'd never have gotten off the ground with Oprah if we hadn't seized our moment in that critical meeting. More often than not, you get only one real chance to make your pitch—so make it count.

CHAPTER 4

Fear

One afternoon during my time as publisher of *New York* magazine, I was scheduled to make a presentation to the magazine's owner, Rupert Murdoch. Murdoch wasn't yet the huge international media mogul he'd later become (though he did own both the *New York Post* and the *Village Voice*), but he was already a powerful and intimidating figure—a multimillionaire newspaper heir with a pit-bull reputation.

Murdoch, who is Australian, had a way of conversing that always left me feeling off balance. Something about the rhythm of his speech, or the way he paused before answering, always kept our conversation from flowing naturally, so that no matter whether we were in a group or talking one-on-one, I never felt totally at ease with him. Smart as a whip, laser-focused, he wasn't one for small talk or pleasantries, and for some reason, earlier in my career I could never break through the strangely stiff feeling that permeated our interactions. My natural exuberance never seemed much of an asset around him.

On this particular day I was scheduled to make a presentation to him in his office at the *New York Post*'s headquarters. We'd just purchased a magazine called *Cue*, and my presentation was about how to incorporate it into *New York* magazine and how much money we'd need to promote it.

I showed up at Murdoch's office with two other executives (one of them my boss), and the three of us were ushered in. We expected to have about an hour with him, and we'd prepared absolutely everything in advance, with visuals and handouts spelling out all the details he needed to know. I'd worked hard, and as I walked in I could feel my adrenaline starting to pump. You always want to make a good presentation, never more than when it's to the owner of your company.

When we entered the spacious room, with its wall of windows facing the East River, Murdoch was sitting behind his desk. He stood up, said a brief hello, then peered over the pair of little half-moon reading glasses he was wearing. "I'm going to remain standing," he said, eyeing us in turn. "I find that when I stand, the meetings are shorter."

We stopped dead. Did Murdoch really want to hear this presentation? We were asking him for a lot of money, and he was obviously instructing us to keep it short. Was he in a hurry, or was there something else at work here? Not knowing him very well, I had no idea what was behind his sudden declaration, and for a moment I wondered whether he was sorry he'd bought the magazine.

I exchanged glances with the other two guys and made a decision on the fly: we would shrink our hour-long presentation into four minutes, and I would handle it.

As Murdoch stood peering over his glasses, I raced through the concept and the numbers, condensing everything and leaving out all the supporting details we'd painstakingly pulled together. It was like giving the Cliff's Notes for a novel instead of delivering a dissertation on it, but I had to assume that that was what he was looking for. I don't think I took a breath until I was finished, but at the end of the four minutes, Murdoch said, "Thank you, Cathie. I understand what you want to do, and why you need the promotional dollars. You've got them."

With that, he sat down—the sign that the meeting was over. I breathed a sigh of relief. Good preparation and a quick decision had carried us through.

Fear—fear of someone's reaction, fear of unexpected consequences, fear of failure—is a very real part of the work experience, and learning how to deal with it is one of the most empowering skills you can develop. In fact, you can learn not only to neutralize the harmful aspects of fear, but to turn it around and use it for your benefit.

Understanding your fears is the first step to conquering them. Let's start with one of the most common: fear of people's reactions, such as rejection, confrontation, or ridicule. When you're facing these feelings, it helps to

---

Sprinkle around the "fairy dust."

This phrase sounds a little silly, I know, but that's partly why I chose it. What do I mean by "fairy dust"? I'll explain with a story from my days at *Ms.*

The "spitting" incident I described in chapter 3 wasn't an isolated experience for those of us at *Ms.* Because we represented a feminist magazine and movement, some men perceived us as a threat and responded with aggression. Sometimes the affronts were mild, nothing more than people ostentatiously peering out of their offices to get a glimpse of the feminist "freaks and weirdos" coming to pitch their magazine (especially when Gloria

Steinem would come on an ad sales call). But sometimes, as with the spitting media director, they were more overt. To a certain extent, we all had to deal with fear, or at least a certain level of anxiety, when going out to represent the magazine.

Once, at a meeting with a major home appliance manufacturer, one of our ad reps was making her pitch when their guy suddenly interrupted her. "This all sounds lovely," he said in a sarcastic voice. "But why would we want to advertise in a magazine for lesbians?" Rude as the question might sound, it was a common refrain from people seeking to pigeonhole the magazine and the women's movement. So *Ms.* publisher Pat Carbine had given our team advice on how to respond to it—advice our ad rep now put into play.

"You know," she replied with a smile, "even lesbians do laundry."

In spite of himself, the guy had to laugh—and so, with six simple words, our ad rep had defused a potentially ugly situation. She had refused to be intimidated by him, and rather than getting up in arms and escalating the situation, she'd calmly used humor to take back control of the dialogue.

This method was a Pat Carbine specialty; it was as if she had some kind of fairy dust she could sprinkle at will to defuse tension. Pat had two vital tools at her disposal: a gift for never overreacting and a ready sense of humor. She almost never gave in to fear or panic, choosing instead to approach difficult situations with good humor, which was also a great method for robbing them of their negative power. Even just thinking of the phrase "fairy dust" is reminder enough not to overreact to a perceived affront.

Eleanor Roosevelt once wrote, "No one can make you feel inferior without your consent." By the same token, no one in the workplace can make you feel fear without your consent. When you make a point of responding to your own fear with a light touch, you can strip it of much of its power. This may sound simple, but give it a try—it really works.

Fear is often related to expectations. Have you ever asked yourself:

- Am I really qualified for the job I've been hired to do?

- Will I make a stupid mistake and let the whole team down, just when they're counting on me?

- Has too much has been put on my shoulders at work, and will I bomb?

During the first part of my career, as I moved up the ladder at *Holiday, Ms.,* and *New York,* I didn't worry much about whether I was qualified or capable enough to do my job. I was lucky enough to have confidence in my abilities, and hadn't ever really been knocked down. It just never occurred to me that failure was an option. Then, when I got into the high-stakes world of *USA Today*—as a top-level executive in a huge, risky startup— I had a sudden and startling introduction to the concept of performance anxiety. In a flash, I had to learn how to

> **Keep your brain working even if your head's on the chopping block.**

In the early days of *USA Today,* almost no one but its founder, Al Neuharth, was convinced it would survive. There were just too many strikes against it, from the relentless drumbeat of negative press to the logistical hardships of trying to distribute a nationwide paper via satellite. Critics derided *USA Today* as a graphics-heavy, content-light whim that would never win enough readers to survive. And the newspaper was burning through money at a rate that couldn't possibly continue for long.

During the paper's tumultuous first year, Neuharth made it work through sheer force of will. This was a startup on a gargantuan scale, and the challenges of persuading advertisers to take it seriously were equally huge. So when I came on board as the newspaper's third president in a year, as an executive with a solid background in national advertising, the hope for the paper's success suddenly rested in large part on my shoulders. Yet I didn't fully realize that fact until two things happened.

First, one day soon after I'd started working at *USA Today's* offices just outside Washington, D.C., I found myself in the elevator with a man I'd never met. He knew who I was, though, and as the doors swooshed shut, enclosing us in that little space together, he turned and said, "You're Cathie Black, right? I just want to tell you how glad I am that you're here!"

"Thank you," I answered, and smiled. *How nice to get such a warm welcome,* I thought.

"Yeah," he said. "My wife and I just bought a new house, and I'm kind of freaked out about my mortgage. I've been really worried that I'll lose my job if the paper fails," he went on, as the elevator doors opened and he started to step out. "But now that you're here, I've got new hope!" With that, he disappeared down the hallway.

Wow. I'd had the experience of hiring and firing people in my career, and somewhere deep down I knew that people's livelihoods depended in part on my performance as an executive. But I'd never thought of it in such stark terms before. Was I really responsible for making sure this guy could meet his mortgage payments? This was a level of responsibility I hadn't considered before, and didn't particularly welcome.

Even so, I didn't spend a lot of time thinking about it until a few months later. *Fortune* magazine was doing a profile of me, and when it came out in their September 3, 1984, issue, I was out of town. I called my assistant, Naomi, and asked, "So, how's the *Fortune* piece look?" She paused for a moment, then said, "You're not gonna like the headline." She read it to me over the phone, and my heart plummeted.

It was this, in large bold type: CAN CATHIE BLACK PULL *USA TODAY* OUT OF THE RED? Not "Can Cathie Black *Help*" pull it out of the red, not "Can *USA Today*'s Advertising Team" pull it out—but can I, Cathie Black, personally rescue this giant, unprofitable, highly criticized newspaper from collapsing under its own weight? Up to this point, I'd assumed the blame would fall on Al Neuharth if *USA Today* failed. But in this one unbelievable moment of reckoning, I suddenly realized it would also fall on me.

For the first time I truly felt a pang of fear. *USA Today* had already lost tons of money and it was steadily losing more— losses the parent company, Gannett, clearly couldn't sustain indefinitely. Persuading reluctant companies to buy advertising in the paper would be, as *Fortune* put it, my "hardest sell ever." "The task she faces as the new publisher of *USA Today* is as dicey as they come," *Fortune* reporter Myron Magnet had written. "After two years on the market and a pretax loss that will approach $250 million by year-end, Gannett Co.'s national newspaper hasn't yet proved it can succeed."

With the publication of the *Fortune* story, it suddenly felt as though all eyes were on me. And for a moment I wondered whether I could fulfill the expectations Neuharth and the Gannett company had placed in me. What would it be like to fail? How would it feel to work insanely hard for the next couple of years, only to see the newspaper fold? Was it really possible to persuade reluctant advertisers to get on board? Could I really succeed in the face of all this skepticism?

The only absolute certainty was this: If I allowed myself to become cowed by the magnitude of the task at hand, my whole team would have a harder time succeeding. For one thing, fear often drives people to change their tactics—instead of *playing to win,* you end up *playing not to lose.* And unfortunately, in a tough work situation where you must project confidence in yourself and your product, playing not to lose is the surest way to lose. So, instead of focusing on how steep my climb would be over the next couple of years, I broke it down into smaller steps.

The best way to neutralize fear is by breaking it into manageable parts. If the next month at work promises to be daunting, focus only on the next week. If the task of pulling your project out of the red is overwhelming, focus on improving the bottom line incrementally. Success builds upon success, so if you can start with small accomplishments and move forward from there, you'll find the whole process less intimidating.

And if you're still in doubt, remember that the consequences of failure—just like the potential consequences of taking a risk— are almost never as terrible as they seem. Just about anyone you can think of who's a huge success today, in any field from business to politics to sports, has overcome failure to get there. Think of Michael Jordan, the greatest basketball player of all time, who was cut from his high school team; or J. K. Rowling, turned down by more than a dozen publishers before one decided to take a chance on her manuscript about a young wizard named Harry Potter. Most highly accomplished people attribute their successes to early failures that motivated them to do better.

Nobody likes to fail, and I'm certainly not advocating it as a strategy. But as these stories show, fear of failure shouldn't paralyze you. Play to win.

HAVE you ever been in a meeting where out of the blue, a colleague starts complaining about your work on a project? Or made a presentation you were really pleased with, only to be stunned later when someone picked it apart? When people express negative opinions about you or your work, how do you deal with it? Do you fear being criticized, either in public or in private?

When someone criticizes you, you're immediately faced with a choice. You can

- take it at face value, admit your shortcomings, and try to learn from it

- defend yourself—after all, just because someone criticizes you, that doesn't make it true

- listen without argument, then continue what you've been doing anyway

Which is the most appropriate response? If you always defer to others' opinions of how you should perform, it might be a sign that you lack confidence in your own judgment. On the other hand, if you refuse to acknowledge legitimate criticism, you miss out on opportunities to improve your performance and your situation at work. So here's the real underlying question: How can you know whether a colleague's criticism is on the mark? I'll tell a pair of stories that will give you some insight into the answer.

> **You can take it or leave it, but don't fear criticism.**

Earlier in this chapter, I described giving a presentation to Rupert Murdoch. It wasn't often that I presented directly to Murdoch, so those instances are pretty well ingrained in my memory. This one is ingrained, too, but for a different reason.

Murdoch had asked me to present the overall business picture of *New York* magazine to the board of his company. So I prepared all my numbers and notes, jotting everything down on index cards and running through the presentation in my head. On the day of the board meeting, I walked into the beautiful dining room with its long, gleaming mahogany table, greeted the six or seven board members including my boss, Marty Singerman, and launched into my presentation. I'd never been asked to present to the board before, and I wanted to do a great job.

Boy, was I *on* that day. I walked the board through the numbers and told them enthusiastically how the magazine was doing and what our plans for it were. You know how you can feel it when you're hitting on all cylinders, really working a room? That's how I felt. When I wrapped up my presentation, I walked out with a confident smile on my face.

The next day, Marty stopped by my office. I was pleased to see him, thinking he'd probably come by to compliment me on my presentation.

"You know, Cathie," he said, "you don't have to sell so hard at a board meeting. The tone of your presentation was a little over the top."

I stared at him for a moment, trying not to react, but inside I was crushed. I'd worked so hard to prepare and deliver a presentation that was brisk, lively, informative. The board had been pleased, hadn't they? Or did Marty Singerman see something I didn't?

I hid my disappointment, but after he left my office, I thought a lot about what he'd said. Was he right? Or would I be better off just brushing off his words and getting on with my day? I needed answers to two questions in order to determine whether Marty's criticism was legitimate or not.

- Could I trust that he was acting in good faith and not on some ulterior motive just to bring me down a notch?

- Did he have some knowledge of this particular situation that I didn't?

Whenever someone criticizes you, ask yourself those two questions, and the answers will tell you everything you need to know. If the answer to both is yes, you should take the criticism seriously, because there's a good chance it's on target. If the answer to either or both questions is no, you'll need to dig a little deeper before deciding whether to stand your ground or heed your critic's words.

In this case, the answer to both questions was yes. Even though I didn't understand what I'd done wrong, I trusted Marty and knew he didn't have a secret agenda where I was concerned. And as I thought more about what he'd said, I realized an important fact: I'd never presented to a board meeting before. Perhaps there was just a different protocol to that type of presentation.

As it turned out, that was exactly the problem. I had approached the board members as I would a potential client, trying to sell them on the company and our product. But corporate board members aren't there to be sold—their purpose is to help guide the company, through good and bad times. And as such, they need to have unvarnished, straightforward information to aid in their decision-making. A board meeting usually has a low-key, businesslike atmosphere, and I had come in, flags flying, with the hard sell. It just wasn't the right approach.

Difficult as it was to accept, the criticism that had stung so much was right on target. So the next time I presented to the board, I remembered Marty's words and tailored my presentation accordingly.

Learning how to accept constructive criticism is a hugely important skill, not only at work but in life. It's easy to take offense when friends or colleagues tell you something you don't want to hear. But ask yourself those two questions, and try to assess things as unemotionally as possible. You'll find that the line between fair and unfair criticism becomes much more distinct.

How should you respond if you feel you're being criticized unfairly? Don't be afraid to

> **Stand your ground when you have the grounds to stand on.**

One criticism that has been directed at me repeatedly over the years is that I hire too many women. The truth is, I do often hire women to fill executive positions, but do I really hire "too many"? How many is too many, anyway, especially if they're all highly qualified?

In 1985 an *Adweek* magazine profile made reference to the criticism I'd taken over this issue:

> The most controversial segment of her career . . . [was] her second tour of duty, first as ad director, then as publisher, at *New York*. "She fired all the men at *New York* and replaced them with women," one disgruntled marketer complains—and that charge was given currency by a *Fortune* profile last year. "I'm very sensitive to those charges, and I'm very aware of them," Black says evenly. "They're not true." Nonetheless, she had no compunction about cleaning out veteran salespeople she thought had gone soft. "I told them, 'We have a new product, the city is different. Either you're going to be on the new team or not, but I don't want to hear about the past all the time.' Some people left, and some were encouraged to leave."

Sound familiar? Just as at Hearst, where I instituted a ten-dollar fine for any employee who said, "We tried that already,"

I wanted my team at *New York* to focus on the future, not on the past. Those who couldn't or wouldn't were soon on their way to other jobs. And as I filled the new positions, it's true that I hired a higher percentage of women than had worked at *New York* previously. Was it legitimate to criticize those hiring choices? Or was this a case when my best response would be to dismiss the criticism?

If you apply the test of the two questions to this particular scenario, the answers are very different from those in Marty Singerman's case. Were the critics acting in good faith, or did they have some kind of ulterior motive? Well, some of the grumbling came from people who'd lost their jobs, and some of it came from those who weren't comfortable with an affront to the status quo. None of it was directed at me with the goal of helping me do my job better, so the answer was clearly no.

As for the second question, did any of my critics have knowledge of the situation that I didn't? The answer to that was clear as well: no. Given those two negative answers, along with my own gut instincts, I knew the criticism wasn't legitimate. I was hiring able and experienced executives, and even though I was hiring more women than my predecessors had, the notion of "too many" struck me as absurd. After all, how many people complain when male executives hire mostly other male executives for their teams? And how close are most executive teams to fifty-fifty gender splits, which would be fairest of all?

When the grumbling about my hiring so many women continued into my tenure at Hearst, I took a page from Pat Carbine's playbook, and decided to sprinkle a little fairy dust in response. The moment I chose was at our annual holiday luncheon for executives, where I stood up after the meal and made some short remarks to nearly a hundred Hearst executives.

It's a lighthearted, celebratory event, so I usually recite a humorous poem or make jokes. This time, though, I said, "Some people seem to think I hire too many women," as I smiled and I looked around the room. "I just want you to know I'm listening to their complaints. So I thought I'd do a little survey. Would all the women executives please stand up?"

The women stood. And as heads swiveled all around the room, people took in the obvious truth: only about a third of the luncheon guests were women. Too many women? Wouldn't that qualify as too few, if anything?

"Thank you," I said, still smiling. "And now, would the men please stand?" With that, the dozens of men in the room stood, solidifying my point better than any harangue possibly could have. People murmured and laughed, and the men sat down. Point made, I sat down, too.

VERY soon after I started working at *USA Today*, Al Neuharth asked me to take part in a 9:00 a.m. meeting at Gannett's Madison Avenue offices. I planned to get there a couple of minutes early, but my phone rang at 8:45 a.m. Neuharth's executive assistant, Randy Chorney, was on the line.

"Cathie," she said, "where are you? The management meeting's about to begin."

"I know," I told her. "It's at nine, right? I'll be upstairs in a minute." I hung up the phone, slightly confused, and hustled to the conference room on the thirty-second floor, a sleek, stylized, gray-walled chamber with black leather chairs and a U-shaped table. When I arrived, at 8:51, everyone was already seated at their assigned spots, looking as though they'd been settled in for hours. As I took my seat, I shivered—it couldn't have been more than about fifty-eight degrees in that room.

That was my introduction to Al Neuharth's managing style: he liked to start meetings early, he liked to keep conference rooms chilly, and he liked to keep people a little off balance.

Sometimes *way* off balance. Neuharth was a great leader in many ways, but he subscribed to the old-fashioned notion that you lead by instilling fear in your employees. As I'd soon find out in this meeting, he sometimes pushed things too far.

Don't wield fear as a weapon.

At precisely 8:57 a.m., Neuharth walked in. Wearing his trademark silk suit and dark sunglasses, with his gray hair neatly swept back, he reminded me of Frank Sinatra. He strode to his place at the head of the table (no one was ever seated next to him at these meetings) and whipped out an envelope.

"What the hell is this?" he demanded, waving the offending object in the air. I couldn't tell what, if anything, was in the envelope, but I could see that it had perforations down the sides, like a sweepstakes mailing. Neuharth looked around the room, his face in a pucker, and theatrically pulled open the perforations.

"This looks like a *medical bill!*" he roared. "Whose stupid idea was this? This is the most *idiotic* idea for a promotional mailing I've ever *seen!*" He furiously crumpled the envelope, the gigantic gem-encrusted ring on his right hand glinting in the light. Then he turned and fired the wadded envelope right at the head of the circulation director, whose department had come up with the offending design. The circulation director flinched, then sat silently with his head down, looking like he was about to be sick.

I glanced across the table at the head of Gannett Media Sales, my new buddy Ray Gaulke. I could tell when our eyes met what he was thinking—because it was exactly the same thing I was thinking.

What the hell had we gotten ourselves into?

Neuharth continued his rant, stalking around the table and broadening his criticism to include not just the circulation director, but everyone in the room. "How are we going to survive if *this* is the caliber of our creative ideas?" he snapped. "We have *got* to do better than this! This paper will *fold,* jobs will be *lost,* and you'll be branded *failures* if we don't focus and perform!" Neuharth glared around the table, as if daring us to speak.

Was Neuharth's atom-bomb approach effective? Yes and no. The circulation director he'd berated so fiercely was given a graceful exit from the company in a matter of months. The ever-present threat of a meltdown from Neuharth—a man who later proudly titled his memoirs *Confessions of an SOB*—struck fear into the hearts of numerous *USA Today* employees. On the other hand, he succeeded in motivating a group of talented, driven executives to overcome historic odds. In many ways he willed *USA Today* into existence through the force of his personality, charisma, and occasionally maniacal leadership.

President Lyndon B. Johnson is said to have defined a leader as "someone who, if you don't do what they say, can do something terrible to you." Perhaps when LBJ was in office in the sixties, the "fear as motivation" tactic was effective, but I don't believe that's true anymore. Today I believe you can get better performance out of your team through a reasoned, balanced approach. Striking fear in your employees might lead to temporarily heightened performance, but over time the damage it does to morale outweighs the benefits.

Whether you're the leader or the follower, the key to creating an atmosphere where productivity thrives is the same:

> **Know the difference between professional and personal provocation.**

When Neuharth threw that crumpled envelope, I could tell by the look on the circulation director's face that he wouldn't survive this kind of atmosphere for long. Maybe that was Neuharth's plan—to weed out anyone who wasn't psychologically equipped for trench warfare. But in my opinion he'd gone too far. There's no need to shock or traumatize your team to make a point, or ridicule someone in front of others.

There was one other memorable occasion when Neuharth pushed as close to the edge as I have ever seen an executive go. This one was so far out there, it was the stuff of legend.

Neuharth would regularly summon USA Today executives to his home in Florida for meetings. It was impossible to predict when the urge might strike him, but we all lived in a state of perpetual readiness to fly down on very short notice. One Saturday evening my husband and I came home after dinner to find a message on my answering machine: "Be at Dulles airport at four p.m. tomorrow." The Gannett corporate planes were housed there in the private jet terminal, so this was the cue that Neuharth was summoning me to Florida. A late Sunday meeting was definitely out of the ordinary, so I was immediately suspicious, and figured this couldn't be good news.

What was this about? Was I being fired? I'd been given no clues, and had no way of finding anything out, at least until I got to the airport the next day and saw whether anyone else was flying down with me.

When I arrived at the airport, a couple of other executives were there, too. This made me feel a little better, although, as we settled into our seats, it was clear everyone was nervous. Was the newspaper folding? Were we all about to lose our jobs? Keeping us guessing was, of course, another of Neuharth's tools for maintaining control. On the flight down, there was only the sound of quiet small talk.

We landed in Florida and were immediately whisked by limo

to Neuharth's home in Cocoa Beach. Called "Pumpkin Center," it's a beautifully renovated house with a pool and tennis court on five oceanfront acres. Though it looks like a log cabin on the outside, the house's interior is more reminiscent of the Playboy Mansion, with huge open spaces and an indoor swimming pool. Once inside, we found a few other executives who'd also been flown down, and soon we were all ushered upstairs to the conference room and seated at a long table made from rough-hewn wood and bark.

A moment later, Neuharth walked in. He looked at each of us and said in a low voice, "If you smart people cannot figure out all the things you're doing wrong, and fix them, this paper is going to go out of business sooner than you can imagine." He continued in that vein for another five minutes, berating us for our shortcomings and painting in stark terms the ever-deepening black hole the paper was in. He concluded with an invitation to dinner. "You're all going to have to figure out how the hell to fix this. But tonight, meet me at the Surf for dinner. We'll start at seven p.m." He then left the room.

Bernard's Surf was the most popular restaurant in Cocoa Beach. Packed with retirees and locals, with the smell of fried fish heavy in the air, it was a far cry from the high-end restaurants many of the executives were used to, but Neuharth was a regular and even had his own table. The other executives and I arrived at the restaurant together, and we were shown into the one private dining room.

The first person to enter the room murmured, "Oh my God." A few more people filed in, and then I reached the doorway. I looked in and beheld the most extraordinary sight I'd ever seen.

Al Neuharth was sitting at the table, dressed in a robe, a crown of thorns perched atop his graying head. With his hand he was steadying a giant wooden cross.

I could not believe my eyes. Had Neuharth lost his mind?

We all knew he was quirky and a little over the top, but when the chairman and CEO of a multibillion-dollar company dresses up like Jesus Christ in a public restaurant (albeit in a private room), there's ample reason to wonder about his sanity. Reaction in the room ran from amusement to shock, and several people who were regular churchgoers were truly offended.

Neuharth's point was that he was giving his lifeblood for the newspaper. He wanted to encourage us to give it our all, too, and he seemed to think that his shocking charade was a way to get us more fired up. But as memorable as Neuharth's gambit was, I don't believe it was worth the ill will it caused among some members of his team.

That time he might have gone too far, but in general Neuharth had an amazing talent for pushing his teams right to the edge but not over it. Fortunately for him, his employees knew how to

> **Use fear as a launching pad.**

One of the most powerful martial arts is judo, a system of self-defense in which you turn your opponent's momentum against him. If your opponent rushes at you, instead of clashing with him head-on, you sidestep and use the force of his charge to throw him off balance. You can do the same thing with fear: instead of fighting it and trying to push back, you can use it to motivate yourself.

Al Neuharth liked to instill fear in the workplace, as a way of lighting a fire under people. Like the stories in his beloved *USA Today*, he didn't waste words, but got right to the heart of things. One succinct, powerful memo he wrote perfectly captures that tone:

> Gannett is *USA Today*, *USA Today* is Gannett. *USA Today* is not Al Neuharth.

USA Today has put the Gannett Company in the major leagues. *USA Today* can keep Gannett there, or it can dump Gannett back in the minor leagues to stay.

You in your forties and fifties had better think about that hard. You will reap the benefit and prestige and stature and [do well] financially or you will suffer the consequences.

Neuharth and [publisher Jack] Heselden will be gone and pretty much forgotten, win or lose. Us guys in our sixties will retire and enjoy life. You in your forties and fifties will live with it, whatever it is. It is *USA Today*.

If it succeeds, you are stars and running a prestigious major-league media company with the flagship, *USA Today*, that is the envy of all. If it fails, you, Gannett, are resigned to being a minor-league outfit . . . for the rest of your career. You have a great opportunity to cash in or to blow it.

The specter of such huge failure might have paralyzed some people, but Neuharth knew his executives well. When he offered us a choice, "Cash in or blow it," we *used* that fear as motivation. No one wanted to fail, so we fought even harder to turn the newspaper around.

Even today, when I read this memo, it makes me want to go out and call on advertisers to sell *USA Today* all over again, to work like hell to overcome the odds we were facing. Launching *USA Today* involved a super-concentrated, Herculean effort, and it was an extraordinary working environment. And because the line between success and failure was so thin, it may well have been our team's ability to use fear as a motivator that made the difference.

So, don't *fear* your own fear. Use it to propel yourself forward. It may well become the best motivator you can find.

BLACK & WHITE

Landing Your Dream Job

I thought I'd seen everything, until the day a giant potted plant appeared in my office at *New York* magazine. It looked about four feet tall.

"What is this?" I asked my assistant. She told me it was from someone I'd just interviewed for a job. She handed me the card that came with it, and I read with astonishment, "I'd love to come work for you and help your garden grow" (or some such), signed by the hopeful job applicant.

Dear God. This was so obviously not the way to get a busy executive's attention, I could hardly believe someone had actually sent it. It's a must to follow up after an interview, of course—but a giant plant? "Can you do something with this?" I asked my assistant, officially marking the end of any "gardening" we'd be doing with that person.

Communicating well with potential employers is a critical factor in building your successful career. Fortunately, there are simple and straightforward ways to do it well. Here are five key elements of the job hunt, whether you're new to the work world, looking to advance, or just want to change companies.

COVER LETTER

1. **Send one.**

    You wouldn't believe how many times I get just a résumé, with no cover letter at all—which always makes me think, *No wonder this person is unemployed.* You may think writing a letter isn't necessary, since all the relevant info is in your résumé. But your cover letter makes a crucial first impression, allowing you to highlight your relevant skills and interest in that company while demonstrating that you're able to communicate well.

2. **Just the facts, ma'am.**

    Make your cover letter short and sweet, no more than one page. This is not the place to wax eloquent about your personal philosophy and childhood dreams. You don't want your potential employer to get impatient wading through multiple pages when what he or she really wants is a quick summary.

3. **Know what to say (and what not to say).**

    The best cover letters express three things: why you're good at what you do, how you'll help the company, and your enthusiasm for the job. Always keep in mind this question: *What does the employer need to know?* It's much more important to show an employer that you'll bring needed skills to her business than to explain how the job fits into the grand scheme of your personal ambitions. Remember, for employers, it's not about you. It's about what you can do for *them.*

4.   Print it (and your résumé) on high-quality paper.

You might think this doesn't make a difference, and perhaps, to a handful of employers, it won't. But why take the chance with cheap printer paper, when it's so easy to use heavier, higher-quality paper? The way you present yourself is an indicator of how you'll represent a company if you get hired, and employers know it. So make sure you're putting out a quality product.

5.   Close by saying you'll call them.

Then do it. Never close a letter with "I look forward to hearing from you." Instead, identify the next step, and make it an active one—something you can do to move the ball forward. It's much better to say, "I'll call your office on Wednesday the 26th to check in," which allows you to push things ahead, rather than waiting for a call that might never come. Then, when you do call, have a copy of your letter in front of you for reference: "I'm calling to follow up on my letter of March 17 . . ."

Résumé

1.   Don't overdo it.

Lots of new trends are popping up with résumés, such as including photos or even short videos (or not so short, as in the infamous case of Yale student Aleksey Vayner, who made an embarrassingly egotistical seven-minute video that ended up on YouTube). But your best bet is to go with something basic. Keep it short—no more than two pages, and just one if you can swing it. Keep it simple—no crazy graphics or hard-to-read fonts. And keep it focused, including just the information that will show an employer your relevant skills and qualities.

2.   Use help to make it great.

There's an art to preparing a great résumé, so don't be shy about asking the experts for help. Books like *The Résumé Handbook* and *Résumés for Dummies* give great tips, or you can hire a professional service to spruce yours up. Your résumé is a hugely important document for advancing your career, so it's worth spending the time and money you need to make it the best it can be.

3.   Spell-check it.

Don't let any misspellings or grammatical errors sneak into either your résumé or your cover letter. Double-check the spellings of names, titles, and companies (remember, the Cathies of the world really hate having their name spelled "Kathy"). And read carefully through each letter before sending it, especially if you're reusing an earlier version of a letter and just filling in the new company information. Recently I got a letter from a job-seeker who had clearly done a global search-and-replace on an earlier letter. How did I know? The word "Hearst" appeared throughout, but everything else in the letter perfectly described our competitor, Condé Nast, where she must also have applied. That's one person who definitely didn't get a call back.

4.   Tailor your résumé to the job you're applying for.

It's fine to have several different versions of your résumé, tailored to different types of jobs, so long as the information remains accurate and the differences are in what you choose to emphasize. Getting a good job is a matter of matching your skills with your employer's needs.

5.   Don't exaggerate—and never lie.

If you went to college but never graduated, don't say—or even imply—that you did. Don't say you worked somewhere for seven years if you were there for five and a half years. Even if you think you can get away with it, resist any temptation to inflate your credentials. It's simply wrong. And you probably won't get away with it, anyway.

Landing and Preparing for the Interview

1. **Be persistent.**

   As I wrote in chapter 1, persistence pays—whether you're hoping to land a job interview, a new account, or anything else. So pick up the phone and call your potential employer to ask where they are in the hiring process, and whether there's anything you can do to help move it along. You don't want to hound them, but it's definitely helpful to show initiative. In that same vein, if a job you want becomes available at your current workplace, don't wait for someone to ask if you're interested. Jump right in and volunteer that you're very interested—you'll be taken much more seriously as a candidate.

2. **Do your research on the company and the person interviewing you.**

   I recently interviewed a candidate to be our new director of human resources, and though I was impressed with her credentials, she'd clearly done no research before the interview. She didn't know much about our magazines or company—not even the basics, such as that I'd been at Hearst for ten years and spent eight years at *USA Today*. Now, I'm not saying she needed to have written a dissertation about my work history, but especially in this age of Google and instant information, it takes only a couple of minutes to get basic facts about a company and an interviewer. If someone comes to interview with me and doesn't know anything about Hearst, I automatically take them less seriously as a candidate. After all, if you don't have the initiative to spend ten minutes preparing for me, how do I know you'll have the initiative it takes to succeed?

3.   **Think about these questions in advance.**

You can almost guarantee that a potential employer will ask you some variation on the following questions:

- What do you want to get out of this position?
- What are the weak spots in your résumé, and how can you address them candidly and succinctly?
- Have you ever been fired? Why?
- What are your strengths and weaknesses?
- Where do you want to be in five years?

THE INTERVIEW

1.   **Look great.**

As discussed in the Black & White section "First Impressions," looking good really does count. You don't have to look like a fashion model, but do dress in clothes that are appropriate.

2.   **Bring a pad of paper and a pen.**

I can't tell you how many times interviewees have asked me for a piece of paper or pen, or both, to jot something down. Each time it happens, I'm amazed. Be prepared for your interview: Invest in a leather folder that holds a pad of paper and pens, and always bring fresh copies of your résumé, even if you mailed one to the interviewer already. If the interviewer doesn't have a copy handy, offer a new one.

3.   Get there fifteen minutes early.

Always allow for traffic jams, parking hassles, and any extra time that might be needed to sign in at the security desk, if there is one. At Hearst, for example, you might find yourself behind a bevy of open-call models at the security desk, all waiting to check in, which could take fifteen extra minutes in itself. Get there early enough to find the right floor, use the restroom, freshen up—whatever you need to do to be ready to present your best self. On the flip side, don't arrive more than fifteen minutes early; if you're sitting in my reception area for a half hour, you're going to get agitated and I'm going to be aware that you're hovering there.

4.   Get answers to your questions.

Every job interview is a two-way street. You're not just convincing an employer that they want you—you're also deciding whether the company or organization is the right fit for you. To that end, make sure you get answers to these questions and any others that are important to your decision:

- What's the outlook for the company?
- Where will you fit in the organization?
- Who will you report to?
- Who will report to you?

Remember my story from the Prologue, when Joe Welty shocked me by saying, "I'm not going to be reporting to you"? Don't let that happen to you.

5.   Don't talk too much, and don't overstay your welcome.

The key thing is to follow your interviewer's cues. If you're sitting in a quiet office, it's best to adjust the volume of your voice accordingly. (Not long ago, after interviewing a woman with Ellen

Levine and Eliot Kaplan, our director of editorial talent, I asked them, "Was she incredibly loud, or was it just me?" They both laughed and blurted, "Yes!") And take cues about when it's time to go, too. If you've been in your interview for more than a half hour, you might say, "I don't know how much time you have— I don't want to overstay my welcome," which lets the interviewer know you're aware of the time you've taken.

6.   Be yourself.

I'm giving a lot of dos and don'ts here, but the most important thing to remember is, be yourself. You have plenty of skills and talents to bring to a job—otherwise the employer wouldn't have brought you in for an interview. Trust in yourself and take a deep breath. You're going to do just fine.

FOLLOWING UP

1.   Send a thank-you note.

Always, always, always send a thank-you note or letter to follow up. You'll come across as both polite and thorough, two qualities any employer looks for in a new hire. It's a good idea to send thank-you notes at other times, too—when you get a bonus or a promotion, or anytime you appreciate something your boss has done, either on the job or off. As a longtime executive I can tell you that all bosses love to get thank-you notes, and the higher up the ladder they are, the less likely they are to receive them. We're human, too, and a sincere note of thanks means a lot.

2.   Choose an appropriate card if you're sending one.

Recently I got a thank-you note from a young woman who'd heard me give a speech. She mailed it to me at Hearst—so far, so good—but when I opened the envelope I couldn't believe what she'd sent. It was a *New Yorker* cartoon showing two people in bed, with a risqué punch line! Not what you want to send to an executive when you're trying to make a good first impression. What was she thinking?

Personally, I prefer typewritten letters to handwritten cards, but everyone's different, so do what you feel is appropriate. I also prefer getting thank-you letters through the regular mail, though increasingly people send such correspondence via email. Your best bet is to find out what the recipient of your letter prefers, so ask her assistant, if she has one.

3.   Make friends with the executive assistant.

When I went to my doctor the other day, I noticed the receptionist was drinking out of a Hearst coffee mug. "Oh," I said, "where'd you get that?" thinking it must have been sent as a magazine promotion. "From your assistant, Pamela," he replied. I shouldn't have been surprised; Pamela is the expert at seeing around the curve. When I asked her about it, she said, "I send coffee cups out all the time, to people who are hard to get through to or get appointments with." The assistant is the gatekeeper, so it pays to be nice to him or her.

4.   No potted plants.

Especially ones that are four feet tall.

CHAPTER 5

Power

When you hear the word power, certain images probably spring to mind: corporate aircraft, corner offices, and cars with drivers. These are the trappings of a certain kind of power, it's true. Yet power isn't just something that's concentrated in the hands of a few business executives, lawyers, or politicians. It's something you can, and should, be able to develop for yourself—no matter where your position happens to be on the professional totem pole.

Start by thinking of power not as something a job title bestows on you, but as something you create for yourself. Even when others are above you in the hierarchy, you can still make yourself an indispensable—and therefore powerful—member of your team. The stories in this chapter will show you how to develop your own power, whether you're an intern, a manager, a freelancer, or an executive. Let's start with a few new definitions!

Power = keeping your eye on the big picture.

After nine months as president of *USA Today*, I was promoted to publisher, with Paul Flynn taking my place as the new president. Paul had a lot of experience in newspaper circulation, so he was in charge of that department, even though I'd hoped and wanted to work on circulation myself. Four months later, when Flynn stepped down, I thought I'd have my chance. The new president, Lee Guittar, wasn't a circulation executive—yet Neuharth made it clear that Guittar would in fact be taking on the circulation as well. This development took me by surprise and frankly irritated me. I had nothing against Lee, who was a very able newspaper executive, but why was I being restricted to ad sales?

I channeled my frustration into a memo to John Curley, the president of Gannett, leaving out the niceties and getting right to the point:

> With an about-to-be-named president, I feel compelled to tell you how I really feel. I'm frustrated. And discouraged. And in doubt as to my near-term growth at Gannett/*USA Today*.
>
> . . . In many ways, I don't see my authority increasing . . . In our brief conversation, I've been told that Lee comes as number two, underneath me. At least that's how Al presented it in Dallas. But does he really? Last year I joined *USA Today* with the title of president—only later to discover it was a title with no authority or responsibility . . .
>
> I now sense that same situation is being repeated. The fact is I'm now a publisher in title only. I'm really

an advertising director with a little circulation promotion thrown in.

Curley passed along my memo to Al Neuharth, who responded angrily. He scrawled furious comments in the margins, writing that my memo was "wasted time" and "full of errors and bullshit." He also noted that although I'd described the memo as "highly personal and confidential," I'd had an assistant type it up. "Nothing any secretary handles is 'highly personal and confidential,'" he wrote. "Type it yourself or talk privately about it."

But it was my final two lines that really enraged him. "You may think I'm bold to lay all this out," I'd written. "But if I don't tell you what I think and how I feel, then I have no one to blame but myself." His scribbled response: "Bold? No. Fucked up? Yes."

Neither Neuharth nor Curley ever gave me the marked-up memo, thankfully. In fact, I didn't even know about it until a 1987 book about *USA Today*'s early years—*McPaper*, by Peter Prichard—reproduced it in its entirety. Aside from the fact that I was shocked Neuharth had given the author permission to reprint the memo, I was taken aback by the stinging vehemence of his comments. I read through them once, my anger rising, then closed the book and didn't look at it again. What was the point? By then the memo was a long-dead issue and certainly not worth dwelling on.

Nearly twenty years later, as I started writing this book, I had a look back at *McPaper* and at the infamous memo, and I found myself surprised at my reaction. Instead of reading Neuharth's comments and boiling, I now realized that he'd made some valid points (albeit crudely). For one thing, it *was* wrong of me to have an assistant type up a confidential memo; if the contents of a memo are truly confidential, you shouldn't reveal them to *anyone,* as it's too easy and tempting for that person then to tell other people. More important, I'd written a memo filled with reasons why I was personally upset about a perceived slight. Why should Al Neuharth have cared about that? It wasn't his job to please my ego or me—his job was to please the analysts on Wall Street and make sure *USA Today* survived.

In my memo, I hadn't offered a single suggestion for how to improve the newspaper, but only suggestions for how to placate my own desire to broaden my responsibilities and move up in the company. I'd lost sight of the big picture, and as a result not only was I dissatisfied, my bosses were dissatisfied with me.

In *McPaper*, Neuharth was quoted offering this observation on the aftermath of the memo episode: "When Cathie went back to concentrating on advertising and quit pretending she could run the whole show, she became a super performer." I'll admit I don't love reading those words even now, but my advertising sales skills were the crucial element to moving *USA Today* forward, and my power within the company was commensurate with how successful I was in that pursuit. In any company, but particularly in a startup as bold and big as *USA Today*, experience and results are what matter most. So while there's nothing wrong with aspiring to higher levels or trying to learn something new, don't forget where your power actually lies.

Which calls to mind another definition of power:

Power = understanding what you can and cannot control.

In chapter 3, I told you about a colleague who had a habit of undercutting me in meetings, and about how I made a vow to focus on the positive aspects of our relationship, which improved our relationship greatly. The lesson in that chapter was that you shouldn't personalize things that aren't personal. But the second, equally important lesson is that you must learn what you can't control—and then not waste time trying to control it. Here are a few more examples, to show you what I mean.

A colleague once offered me some unsolicited but extremely insightful advice about Victor Ganzi, who became my boss in June 2002. "I'm going to tell you one important thing, Cathie," she said. "Just remember: You cannot outwork Vic. He works seven days a week and rarely takes a vacation."

Vic might not work seven full days every week, but he really does work at least six, and usually six and a half. It would have been easy for me to feel that I had to match his hours to prove my dedication to the job, but that wasn't necessary. How people work, and how much they work, is very much a part of their own DNA. The only thing you can control is your own schedule and your own rate of production. So, while you should strive to get your work done efficiently, don't ever feel that you have to work crazy hours just for the sake of it.

In any office environment, there are many factors you can't control—the trickiest of which are often interpersonal. People get on each other's nerves, step on each other's toes, vie for each other's jobs, and sometimes, at the other end of the spectrum, get inappropriately involved with each other. At one point much earlier in my career, I had a married boss who was having an affair with a subordinate of his—an awkward situation that made all of our lives more complicated, but about which I could do nothing. It would have been easy to get upset about the situation, but to what end? The only thing you can do is accept what you can't change and work around it. That allows you to have a modicum of power over it.

This isn't meant to imply that you should accept all situations without complaint, however. Sometimes you do have to stick your neck out in an effort to make positive change. The trick is in figuring out when to pick that battle, because

> **Power = choosing your battles carefully.**

Hearst is a privately held company with a long, rich history. Seven of our magazines—*Cosmopolitan, Town & Country, Good Housekeeping, Redbook, Popular Mechanics, House Beautiful,* and *Harper's Bazaar*—are more than one hundred years old. We're proud of our heritage, but we also have to keep up with the demands of a changing, twenty-first-century marketplace.

The most visible symbol of Hearst's push into the future is our new building in midtown Manhattan. Designed by the renowned architect Lord Norman Foster and completed in 2006, the Hearst Tower is, fittingly, a skyscraper built on the foundation of the historic landmark six-story Hearst building at 300 West 57th Street. It was the first skyscraper to break ground in New York after the attacks of September 11, 2001, and the first "green" building in the city to meet the highest environmental standards of Gold LEED certification. With its sleek glass and steel façade, open café, fitness center, and state-of-the-art design elements, it's truly a building for the future.

During the building's design phase, every possible component was pondered, discussed, and debated. From office sizes to floor assignments to bathrooms, every detail came under scrutiny, including, memorably, the Good Housekeeping dining room, a cornerstone of the original Hearst building.

The original Good Housekeeping dining room, with its attendant living room, was famous. Decorated with antique furnishings, a remarkable collection of eighteenth-century glass rolling pins, and first editions of cookbooks, it was an elegant, living monument to history. Over the years, the biggest names in the media, political, and entertainment worlds had attended high-powered events and meetings there, and its aura had been burnished over time.

Given the futuristic feel of the new tower, some at Hearst didn't think it made sense to re-create the traditional Good Housekeeping dining room and living room. And though I was very involved in the plans for the building, I hadn't paid close attention to the placement and design of the dining room—until one day when a group of us met to review the plans and do a walk-through of the new Good Housekeeping Research Institute floor, where the dining room would be located.

My boss, Vic Ganzi, was among those in the group. We moved slowly around the floor in a pack, looking at the various design touches and debating the finer points of carpet colors. When we got to the area where the new Good Housekeeping dining room was to be, I could see Vic begin to tense up.

The beautiful, paneled living room had been eliminated in favor of an open area, and the dining room itself had taken a turn toward the modernistic glass and steel that characterized the rest of the building. The flawless antique flavor that had made the original room so special was gone. Vic turned to me and said, "Well, if this is what you want the Good Housekeeping dining room to be, that's all right." His face was impassive, like a slab of stone. "But I'll never come to it."

Then Frank Bennack, vice-chairman of the board and Vic's predecessor as Hearst CEO, chimed in. "Every sitting president of the United States in our lifetimes, with the exception of Bill Clinton and George W. Bush, has sat in the Good Housekeeping dining room," he announced. "It's a piece of our history. But if *this* is what you all want . . ."

I wasn't in charge of the building plans, but it was clear what the next step needed to be. I urged Lord Foster's architectural team to rethink the plan, restore the living room, and revert to the original design of the Good Housekeeping dining room. Perhaps it would be less architecturally consistent. Maybe it represented an incongruous nod to the past in a building dedicated to the future. But this was one battle that I knew immediately we should not fight. I simply took in the message of what my bosses wanted, and did my best to see that it was fulfilled. With construction so far along, redrawing a floor was an expensive and time-consuming proposition, but it was absolutely worth it.

How do you respond when

- someone at work offers an opinion you disagree with?

- your colleagues make a decision you feel isn't helpful?

- your team begins to move in a direction you believe is misguided?

- your boss swoops in to override a decision you've made?

The simplest answer would be to respond to all these situations by voicing your disagreement. But you'll put yourself in a much more powerful position if you take time to decide when to respond, and when to let something lie. Ask yourself how serious the consequences will be, and how likely you are to succeed in changing your colleagues' minds. Will your energy and time be more profitably spent on more pressing matters? Does it make sense to save your political capital for a more important battle? Consider all these questions before making your move, because no battle is worth fighting just for the sake of the fight.

As you can see, power within the workplace is often closely tied to control. And I don't mean controlling what others do—I mean controlling what you choose to do. Here's another example:

> **Power = controlling the flow of information.**

On my very first day at *USA Today*, I went in quite early to find my office and get settled in. I'd never even seen my office before, since it was in the *USA Today* headquarters in Washington, D.C., while all my interviews had taken place in New York, so I had to ask someone how to get there. So I was pretty surprised when I walked into the reception area and discovered a man sitting there.

"Hi, Cathie," he said, as he jumped from his chair and stuck out his hand. He told me his name, informed me he was a Wall Street analyst, and said, "I'm interviewing Al Neuharth in about an hour. Would you spend some time with me before that? I'd love to ask you a few questions."

"Are you kidding?" I said. "Listen, this is my first day on the job—I don't know anything yet. If I'm stupid enough to talk to a Wall Street analyst this morning, I'll be fired by this afternoon. Sorry!" He laughed, and I hustled past him down the hall.

An hour or so later, Al Neuharth called me. "Cathie," he said, "you didn't tell that analyst anything, did you?" I reassured him that I hadn't said a word. Why would I want to spout off on my first day, when I was still learning the lay of the land? "Good," he said, seeming pleased.

Within a short time, though, I felt more confident in my grasp of the numbers, advertiser reactions, and the business in general. So when the management team of Gannett and *USA Today* was invited to present at a media conference for those same Wall Street analysts, I was one of the executives asked to participate. Al Neuharth, always a savvy and humorous presenter, gave a lively talk peppered with jokes and a few slides showing Gannett's outstanding financial picture over many years. Afterwards we all filed out of the auditorium to go to the closing reception.

When I stepped out into the hallway, I was suddenly surrounded by at least two dozen attendees, all barking questions at me: "When is the paper going to be profitable, Cathie?" "How are your advertising numbers looking?" And that classic Wall Street query, "What's the next quarter going to look like?"

Neuharth saw me in the middle of the scrum and immediately bounded over. He grabbed my elbow and whispered a single sentence in my ear. "Cathie," he said, "don't tell them more than you know."

Neuharth knew it was human instinct for people to want to look as though they have all the answers. Yet, as simple as his advice was, it's the kind of thing that's very easy to forget in the moment. As soon as Neuharth whispered those words, I made doubly sure I didn't go out on any limb—a move that would protect me from saying anything I'd regret or making an unfounded promise. More important, it would protect the company from the fallout of whatever naïve thing I might have been inclined to say.

There's also an important corollary to "Don't tell them more than you know." It's this: "Don't tell them more than they've asked for." Whether you're dealing with a reporter, an analyst, or a potential client, don't run off at the mouth about twenty-seven different topics if someone asks you a direct question. For one thing, you might talk yourself into trouble; I've seen sales reps talk themselves into and right back out of a sale because they couldn't stop nattering on about irrelevant side issues. And for another thing, you might reveal information that you'd be better off keeping to yourself. So keep a lid on it, and keep control of your information.

ALL these suggestions are useful when you're dealing with others in the workplace. Yet power is not just about your external relationships. It's also about the relationship you have with yourself.

Have you ever noticed how, when some people enter a room, the energy seems to change? Certain people radiate self-confidence and charisma, and everyone else in the room can sense it. No matter where they might be on the office hierarchy, they possess what seems to be an innate power to have a positive effect on others.

Where does this power come from? Is it something you're born with or something you can develop? Although some fortunate people really do seem to have been born with charisma, I believe you can develop your own through honing your self-confidence and personal power. And it's not as difficult as you might think. Start with this idea:

Power = knowing your strengths and weaknesses.

A few months ago, a very well-known and successful clothing designer—a man who has conquered the fashion world—was scheduled to attend a formal dinner in Manhattan. The day of the event, he had his assistant call the organizers. A well-known former member of the presidential cabinet was scheduled to attend the dinner as well, and the designer had a special request: he wanted to ensure he wouldn't be seated next to that person. As it turns out, the world of politics was simply outside his comfort zone, and he didn't want to put himself in a situation that might prove an embarrassment. The designer knew what he was good at and what he wasn't, and he took special care to make sure he wouldn't expose his narrow range of conversation topics in a public setting, where they might damage his image.

This might seem an extreme example of strategically masking your shortcomings; after all, the designer lost an opportunity to meet a fascinating person and push his own boundaries. But the basic underlying lesson is still valuable. Know what you're good at and what you're not. And if you are able to work on your weaknesses and play up your strengths, the benefits both at work and in your life will be enormous.

For my part, I've always been drawn to the marketing, sales, and creative side of the publishing business. I also like operations and analysis, but too much data and too many spreadsheets make my eyes glaze over. I'm not hopeless at it; I'm just better at overall strategy than at analyzing spreadsheets. So over the years I've taken care to work on that weakness—taking financial management courses, asking for help when I need it, and not being afraid to let the numbers folks do the thing they're best at. It wouldn't make sense for me to pretend I'm a whiz where I'm not. But what does make sense is playing up your strengths and making sure your team knows where you can add the most value.

The way others perceive you is a huge component in the calculus of power, so don't be afraid to try to influence people's perceptions. Yet, with that in mind, also remember this:

> Power = not getting overly caught up in the
> idea of power.

We're getting to this lesson not a moment too soon, because too much talk of power makes me uncomfortable. I always hesitate a little when anyone asks me about my "power" at Hearst or in the magazine business. It's certainly not the reason I do what I do, and frankly, in many ways it's incidental to what I do.

Jeff Immelt, the chairman and CEO of General Electric, has a similar reaction to the idea of power. He breaks it down this way: "I never sought power. But I understand that I have a powerful job." The distinction is crucial. Buying into the idea that you're personally powerful is the quickest way to lose perspective. Power might be a side effect of your success, but it shouldn't be the ultimate goal. If you seek power for its own sake, you'll succeed only in distancing yourself from your management, your team, and your goals. But if you do your job well, focus on your strengths, and work on your weaknesses, you'll naturally accrue power along the way. Just remember to keep a balanced perspective.

One of my favorite quotes about keeping perspective is a comment by *USA Today*'s Charles Overby. We were at one of the numerous lavish parties that accompanied the newspaper's launch, and he was bustling around, making sure everything was running smoothly. I made some remark about how he was doing all the busywork, and he paused for a moment before turning to me with a theatrical air.

"I, too, have refilled the shrimp bowl," he intoned dramatically.

I laughed, but that quote has stuck with me all these years. What Charles was really saying was that there's no job too big and no job too small, regardless of how high you move up the career ladder. I feel the same way—I'm happy to pitch in to get a room prepared for a meeting or event, and when I see empty coffee cups or crumpled napkins in a meeting room, I don't summon someone else to take care of it, I just clean it up myself. The basic message is this: Don't let an increase in power lead to a swelled head.

In a similar vein, it helps to remember not to take yourself too seriously. You're bound to make mistakes—we all do—and believe me, you'll gain much more respect if you can laugh at yourself than if you become easily flustered and sullen. Being in a position of power doesn't mean you can't be human. In fact, the more grounded you can be about an embarrassing or difficult situation, the more your team will relate to you and be motivated to work for you.

Oddly enough, just as I was writing this chapter I had an incredibly embarrassing moment at a meeting of the Coca-Cola board's compensation committee, which I chair. And as we were wrapping up our two-hour meeting, my back was feeling sore—so I decided to take a couple of Advil. I fished around in my purse, pulled out my little pill case, grabbed a couple of white pills, and washed them down. Just as I was swallowing, I realized that those pills weren't Advil at all—they were Ambien, a powerful sleeping medication I had left over from an overseas trip, which I occasionally took to combat jet lag.

Whoops. I looked around the room, where about eight other board members and staff were gathered. I knew we had another meeting coming up, and then a dinner scheduled for that night. But I also knew I'd be missing both of them, as I'd be fast asleep in about twenty minutes and probably wouldn't wake up until morning.

Feeling sheepish, I slipped a note to the Coca-Cola CEO, Neville Isdell, who quickly arranged for an escort and car back to my hotel. In the meantime I wobbled down the hall to a secretary's office and called a doctor, who reassured me that I'd be fine but completely conked out for many hours. And that's exactly what happened. So much for getting caught up in the idea of power! The only thing I got caught up on that night was my sleep.

Power = knowing you don't have to throw bombs.

Have you ever had a boss who

- fired half the team as soon as she started her job, just to show her muscle?

- switched people's positions around, not because it made sense strategically, but because he wanted to make his mark?

- took great pains to assign blame to subordinates when her project failed?

Some people seem to believe that true power is expressed by cracking the whip, often publicly. But I'd argue the opposite. True power is motivating a team and meeting your goals *without* having to crack the whip. It's having the confidence—both self-confidence and the confidence of your team—to make things happen without needing to browbeat.

When I first started at Hearst, I already knew we needed to "blow the dust off the curtains." The company had a reputation as steady but staid—just a step away from complacent. We needed an infusion of new energy, and part of the reason I was hired was to provide it. Yet I didn't storm in with bazookas blazing. The last thing I wanted to do was come in and shake things up just for the sake of shaking, which would have led to upheaval and mistrust on the part of Hearst management. Instead, I began getting to know people by asking questions and listening, moving deliberately rather than rushing in with my own agenda. In fact, I moved slowly enough that snarky little news items soon began appearing in New York media, asking what I was doing in my new position, and what in the world I was waiting for.

I didn't mind the arrows flying at me in those first few months, because I knew that in time the changes we'd undertake at Hearst would be apparent to everyone. Of course, a part of me wanted to respond to my critics, to show them I had every intention of making the kinds of changes the company needed. But what's more important—making changes according to the critics' timetables or making changes in a way that will most benefit the company? Put that way, it's a no-brainer—no matter the temporary discomfort you might feel.

Kate White, the editor-in-chief of *Cosmopolitan*, calls this approach the "slow burn." Rather than rushing in, making rash decisions that may turn out to be ill-considered, take the time to move ahead slowly and steadily. And when things don't happen to go your way, remember this next lesson.

```
┌────────────────────────────────────────────┐
│   Power = knowing how to let things go.      │
└────────────────────────────────────────────┘
```

Earlier in this book, I wrote about making your life a "grudge-free zone," because while it may feel natural and sometimes even necessary to hold a grudge, the only person it will hurt in the end is you. And the same is true of another pervasive emotion: regret.

When you make a mistake, do you have trouble letting it go? Have you ever spent days, or even weeks, berating yourself for having screwed something up? If so, you're hardly alone—especially if you're a woman. While men tend more often to blame external factors for failed projects, women tend to blame themselves. No one wants to make a mistake, of course, but we all do. So the key is to move on quickly, and not wallow in self-defeating regret.

I've made all kinds of mistakes on the job—some of them real doozies. And I've worked with plenty of bosses who had no qualms about telling me exactly what I'd done wrong, in blunt and vivid terms. If I needed three days to get over every day I was criticized, I'd never have gotten anything done in my career. Not only does it waste time and energy, it also colors how others see your mistake—and, by extension, how they see you. If you stay torn up over a mistake, others will assume it was worse than it probably was. But if you move on quickly, minimizing the damage, you'll have power over how the mistake is perceived by others.

When Condé Nast, one of our competitors, launched an edition of *Glamour* magazine in the United Kingdom, I believed our British version of *Cosmopolitan,* for decades a huge success in that market, would keep its lead. In a speech to a large gathering of *Cosmo*'s international editors (we publish fifty-seven different international editions today), I made a flip remark saying that British *Cosmo* would crush British *Glamour* like "a little armadillo on the road." I knew my offhand comment was sharp and smart-assed, but what I didn't foresee was that someone would leak it to the press. It definitely wasn't something I wanted to see in print! And to make matters worse, when British *Glamour* did become successful, the remark was then quoted as an example of hubris on my part.

It wasn't my finest moment. I had underestimated our competition, and it would have been easy to feel bad about it. Yet it ultimately doesn't help anyone if you dwell on your mistakes or berate yourself. Instead, when you make a mistake, take note of what you might have done differently, and learn what you can to avoid making the same mistake again.

Important as it is to grant yourself leeway to recover from a mistake, it's even more important to grant it to others. If someone on your team screws up, it might well be useful to admonish that person (as we'll explore in the following section). But, more important, you should urge them to ask the essential question, "What can we learn from this?" Why not make your response to mistakes constructive rather than destructive? It will help your team's morale and make it easier for everyone to move forward. Make your workplace—and your life—a regret-free zone.

The deeper we get into this book, the more you'll find that these lessons apply just as much to your personal life as your work life. Learning not to beat yourself up over mistakes is a skill that will enrich much more than just your hours at the office. It will affect how you feel about yourself on the most basic level. The more you can approach your own decisions and accomplishments with a positive attitude, the happier you'll be, and everything else grows from there.

YOU'VE probably heard Theodore Roosevelt's admonition "Speak softly, but carry a big stick" many times. But have you ever thought about how it applies to the workplace? As discussed in the stories above, it's best to wield power in the office carefully, with a view to lifting people up rather than knocking them down. Yet you can't simply be gentle without first establishing a foundation of power and confidence, or you'll end up with chaos. Use your power wisely, but

> **Don't be afraid to bust someone.**

Not long ago an editor was in my office, talking about her magazine and its business metrics. She went on and on, describing trends, data, research, demographics, other magazines—whatever popped into her head. The discussion, if you could call it that, was unfocused, and a waste not only of her time but of mine.

"Stop!" I finally snapped. "Listen to yourself! You're talking about everything under the sun except the readers, when they should be your primary concern. You need to focus on who you're writing and editing this magazine for—not a bunch of gobbledygook about the trend *du jour.*"

She stared at me for a moment, stunned into silence. She obviously felt my interjection was harsh, but I'd used that tone intentionally. I needed to jar her into the realization that her approach was wrong, and telling her gently just wouldn't have had the same effect. And though she might not have liked it, it accomplished what we needed: she stopped hiding behind consumer research and began to see readers as people.

I don't often use a harsh tone, in large part because I rarely need to. People who work with me know I'll come down on them if necessary—but they also know that (1) I won't do so unless it's truly warranted, (2) I won't hold it against them if they make a mistake, and (3) when they do make a mistake, I'll tell them right away, in private. Over the years I've found that maintaining this balance is the best and fairest way to keep people on track and motivated.

Al Neuharth, not surprisingly, was a master at keeping people on their toes. He liked to check in at random times, to ensure we were producing what was expected of us. Valerie Salembier tells a classic story where Neuharth was prepared to bust her and she was forced to wait anxiously to see if he'd have reason to.

In an effort to boost *USA Today*'s revenue from classified ads, Valerie's art director had redesigned those pages to feature, prominently, a toll-free number that readers could call to place ads. One afternoon at a meeting, Neuharth asked her offhandedly how the 800-number promotion was working out. "Great!" she told him. "It's up and running. Everything's going well."

"Okay," he said, "let's see just how well." He began dialing the number on speakerphone, as Valerie and two other ad team members sat frozen at the table. The 800 number *was* working just fine, but now Neuharth's opinion of it would rest on the shoulders of one random person at a faraway phone bank, who would have no idea it was the chairman and CEO of the company who was calling. Valerie held her breath as Neuharth waited patiently. The phone rang . . . and rang . . . and rang. No one picked it up.

"I must have dialed the wrong number," Neuharth said, a slight edge to his voice. "No answer, no recording. Let me try again."

By this time, Valerie was looking sick. Neuharth dialed again, and on the second ring an operator picked up and answered in a polite, cheery voice. Neuharth smiled. And the rest of us around the table breathed a huge sigh of relief. Bullet dodged.

All of us at *USA Today* knew that at any moment Al Neuharth might call or pop in and push our buttons about whatever we were working on. He wasn't the type who would simply ask and take someone's word for it—he wanted to see for himself. It's why he always went directly to whoever was responsible, not caring a whit about reporting structure or protocol. Sure, it was nerve-racking at times, but it also helped keep us working at a highly productive level.

Take power into your own hands.

Have you ever felt that you could run things better than your superiors? Or that you had great ideas for improving the work, if only someone would listen? What do you do when you see a need in the office that isn't being filled, and you have an idea for how to fill it? You can't simply vault past your boss and take charge of everything, of course. But there's a lot you can do that doesn't involve undercutting your boss or overstepping your boundaries. And by taking initiative to improve certain areas of the workplace, you'll make yourself that much more valuable to the team.

During my first year at *USA Today,* I noticed there was a real distance between the newspaper's advertising team, which I headed, and the rest of the paper's staff. While the ad team members had come from all over—other magazines, newspapers, advertising agencies, and the like—the editorial and circulation people had mostly come from within the parent company, Gannett. So, culturally, we were always the outsiders.

This wasn't usually a big deal, but it did become an annoyance during Gannett's annual management meetings. Each year, for a few days in early December, Gannett's senior executives, from general management to divisions from across the nation, gathered to talk about the company's future. There was always a whole schedule of back-to-back meetings, dinners, and receptions, but for some reason, on opening night there was no dinner planned that included the *USA Today* advertising executives. So while everyone else—including those *USA Today* managers who'd originally come from other Gannett properties—had someplace to go, the ad team was left out in the cold.

My first year, after having dinner with three colleagues, I thought to myself, *This is a waste of management resources.* I knew there had to be a better alternative, and I saw three options. I could (1) do nothing, and just dine with my colleagues again at next year's meeting, (2) complain to Gannett about the oversight, or (3) take matters into my own hands and create a solution.

I chose the third option. The next year, when the management meeting rolled around, I invited a mixed group of all the "orphans" from the Gannett events to a party at my home. People were happy to have a place to go, and happy to feel a part of something. It was a really nice evening, so the next year I repeated the dinner, inviting more people and groups. Pretty soon the party was one of the hits of the management week meetings—and not only was it fun, but it brought people together. So while the old saying might be "If you can't beat 'em, join 'em," the new twist is "If you can't join 'em—take action and throw your own party."

• • •

NOT everybody will like it when you take matters into your own hands, but if what you're doing will ultimately help the company and/or your co-workers, don't let the skeptics intimidate you. Just remember that the more innovative you are, the more vocal your critics will be.

At the end of my first year at Hearst, I said to our public relations head, Deb Shriver, "I'd love to put together a really great weekend for our female advertising clients—something with intellectual content and exciting programming. Not just a spa weekend, but a really stimulating getaway." The model I had in mind was the Renaissance Weekend in Charleston, South Carolina, an annual gathering where hundreds of political and business leaders, thinkers, and creative types meet to discuss ideas and make contacts.

For decades, corporate America has offered all kinds of male-oriented, customer-focused getaways. Golf trips, hunting trips, Super Bowl trips—you name it, it's been done. I envisioned this as a place where senior-level women would be mentally stimulated by great speakers, while sharing the ups and downs of work and home life. Despite the gains women have made in the workforce over the last twenty or so years, I believed that even powerful women would benefit from a place where they could really let their armor down and be spiritually refreshed.

So Deb and I put together a conference called Mind, Body, Soul—a three-day getaway with speakers, music, and presentations in a relaxing, resort-type atmosphere at the Delano Hotel in Miami Beach. We invited female editors and publishers from Hearst, and female advertising clients, because we wanted it to be not only personally rejuvenating, but a smart business investment as well. Over the years we've had plenty of inspiring women take part, including singers Melissa Etheridge and Pink, playwright and activist Eve Ensler, writer Naomi Wolf, and political consultant Dee Dee Myers. And I'll tell you something—

we've done it four times now, and every time it has been magical. There's something about checking your baggage at the door and letting yourself open up within a group of female peers that is incredibly energizing. Our executives and clients love it.

Fortunately, most of the men at Hearst—especially the younger guys—thought it was a great idea. But a couple of quite senior execs really didn't like the idea of a women-only event. Why exclude the men? After all, if women rightfully object to male-only events, how can they get away with having an exclusive event of their own?

It's easy to second-guess yourself—to wonder, *Do I really know what I'm doing here, or are these guys right?* So how do you stand up for yourself in the face of push-back?

The answer, as discussed in chapter 2, is to keep your eye on the end game. Ask yourself this: Is the result of your undertaking ultimately helpful to the company? In this case, it clearly was. While the Mind, Body, Soul conference might have irritated a few male colleagues, its bottom line was indisputable—the women who attended, both associates and clients, found it incredibly useful and energizing. On another level, we established relationships with our clients that were meaningful and productive, which led to new business and new accounts for our magazines. We were also offering something these women couldn't experience on their own, and as a result they felt energized not only about their lives and careers, but about Hearst as well.

This was the position I took in discussions with the men who objected, and I refused to waver. When one of them wouldn't let it go, I said, "Look, you attend getaways for the guys, and this is no different. Let's agree to disagree, and move on." And we did. We've never discussed it again. If I'd waited for his permission or approval, I'd still be waiting.

One final note about power: you have more of it in the workplace than you probably think you do. When you comment on others' performance or ideas, your words really do carry weight. Over the years I have learned to

---

Respect the power of words.

Ask yourself these questions:

- Have you ever sent an email lashing out at someone in anger, only to wish later you'd waited until you cooled down?

- Has a colleague ever taken seriously a remark you meant as a joke? Or have you ever told a slightly edgy joke that offended others?

- Have you ever made flip comments to colleagues that could be misconstrued as carrying hidden messages, causing confusion or resentment?

At a holiday dinner earlier this year with Hearst executives and spouses, I gave lighthearted remarks that included an off-color crack about male behavior. The line got a chuckle, but as I reflected on it later, I thought it was not quite the right thing to have said, particularly in a large group setting.

How you express yourself is the key to how others perceive you—and it's completely within your control. So take the time to consider not only what you want to say, but how you want to say it. And remember that words have the power to injure, confuse, and anger—even if you don't mean for them to.

Talk Magazine

It was August 2, 1999, and the sun had just begun to set over Manhattan as I boarded a ferry packed with party guests, ready for a short cruise across New York Harbor to Liberty Island. As our boat neared the tiny island where the Statue of Liberty stands sentry with her torch, I could see that hundreds of Japanese lanterns had been lit, casting a warm glow around the grounds. It was magical. When the ferry docked, we walked off the boat and into the most hotly anticipated party of the decade.

This was the launch party for *Talk,* editor Tina Brown's super-hyped magazine—her first big venture since her huge success editing *The New Yorker* and *Vanity Fair* through the 1980s and 1990s. In those years, Tina had established herself not only as a gifted editor, but as a heat-seeking missile with an uncanny knack for creating buzz. She—and by extension the magazines she edited—exuded an air of elegance, intelligence, and wit. She always managed to draw the brightest stars of the day into her orbit.

Strolling around Liberty Island in the balmy August air, I watched as celebrities like Brad Pitt, Madonna, Demi Moore, Queen Latifah, and Kate Moss mingled with cultural figures like Tom Brokaw, Michael Eisner, Barry Diller, and Henry Kissinger. It was Hollywood meets New York—the perfect melding of style and substance. Hearst was a fifty-fifty partner in *Talk,* along with Disney and its Miramax film division, headed by movie moguls Harvey and Bob Weinstein, and on the eve of the magazine's launch, we all had soaring hopes for it. At the party that night, it was easy to see why.

Two and a half years later, with tens of millions of dollars down the drain, I stood in the offices of *Talk* to deliver the news every staffer dreaded hearing: the magazine was closing down.

"We've tried everything," I told the group of writers, editors, art directors, and support staff, many of whom were visibly upset. "But we're just not getting the traction we need. Ad pages are coming in, but the newsstand sales are hugely disappointing. And unfortunately the costs are exorbitant." I paused for a moment, then lowered the boom. "We've had many conversations with our partners at Miramax and have decided not to invest any more money. I'm sorry." It's a terrible feeling to tell hardworking, talented people that they're suddenly out of jobs, and as I looked around at everyone's faces, including Tina's (whom we'd told earlier in the day), I could feel the anger and disappointment crackling in the room.

What happened in the twenty-eight months between the magazine's launch and its close? What, if anything, could have been done differently to save *Talk*? Most important, what are the lessons we can take away from that painful, very public experience? In the immediate aftermath of the magazine's shutdown, I didn't dwell on those questions, but now it's worth looking back to find the answers.

From the beginning, *Talk* was unlike any other new magazine Hearst had been involved in. For one thing, we got involved late in the game, after Tina Brown and Harvey Weinstein had made many of the preliminary decisions, including what the magazine would be, who the target audience was, and how certain business deals were structured. Hearst's role was to take care of circulation management, subscription fulfillment, newsstand distribution—essentially to make the trains run on time. So right from the beginning we had very little say in the actual editorial product. Lesson one: Don't put up half the money if you aren't an equal partner in the creative rights.

We went into the deal with our eyes open, but, in hindsight, we should have restructured the contract at the outset. Being hands-off on the editorial side went against Hearst's usual practices. Why were we willing to make an exception for *Talk,* when we hadn't done that with two other joint ventures, *Marie Claire* and *Smart Money*? Frankly, Hearst management had always hoped to have Tina as one of our high-profile editors, but the right magazine opportunity never seemed to present itself. Now, with *Talk,* we let ourselves get caught up in the buzz surrounding Tina, who'd spun gold out of glossy magazine pages for so long.

We got caught up in the excitement that surrounds Harvey Weinstein, too. The combination of his clout in Hollywood, plus Tina's editorial chops, promised at first glance to result in a fantastic magazine. But we ignored the most critical rule in developing new projects:

Be discerning, not dazzled.

No matter how sexy a new idea is, no matter how many celebrities are involved, and no matter how much the media may fawn over it, none of these things guarantees its ultimate success. In the magazine world, only three factors determine success or failure: circulation growth, advertising paging, and cost control. These are just about the least sexy metrics you can imagine, but they're the only ones that count, because if not enough people buy the magazine, and not enough companies pay to advertise in it, there won't be enough money to sustain it. It's that simple.

Anytime we consider launching a new magazine at

Hearst, we have to approach it in a completely agnostic way. The question should never be *Do we like it?* It should always be *Is this a great idea? Can it succeed?* And, no less important, *How soon can it succeed?*

The same should be true for you when you assess projects, goals, potential hires—anything and everything of consequence in the workplace. If you go for flash over substance—for example, hiring the big-name consultant just for his name, rather than the smaller one with the better proposal—you'll be sorry in the end. Making decisions based on hype rather than homework invariably results in wasted time, effort, and energy.

Let me be clear: hype is not always bad. Having an air of excitement and buzz surrounding your project can be hugely helpful—buzz means attention, and attention usually means increased sales. Just don't allow the siren song of the buzz to keep you from paying sufficient attention to the basics.

With all this in mind, where did *Talk* go wrong? On the surface, all factors pointed to success. But, looking deeper, the magazine faced real obstacles from the outset—obstacles we might have seen more clearly if we hadn't been quite so caught up in the hype. For one thing, *Talk* had a pronounced New York–Hollywood sensibility, even though we needed it to sell well in markets across the entire country. Tina was so enmeshed in the world of hip New York parties, theater, and media circles that she went overboard on the assumption that the readers wanted that, too. The best example of this was the month when, at the last minute, she made a snap decision to put the Broadway hit *The Producers* on the cover. It was a cover that was sure to appeal to New Yorkers and theater buffs, but the rest of the country had hardly even heard of the play yet. As we found out the hard way, what succeeds in Manhattan doesn't necessarily sell in Memphis.

Another problem was that *Talk*'s partnership with Harvey Weinstein and Miramax films, which was viewed as "synergy" by those inside the magazine, was viewed with suspicion by those outside it. The idea was that content could flow freely between the partners—Miramax could take stories from *Talk*'s pages to create movies, while *Talk* could cover Miramax films and the movie business from an inside perspective. But the relationship drew criticism from the start: Was Tina allowed to give *Talk* an independent editorial voice, or was it a PR mouthpiece for Miramax?

Also, while Tina and her staff worked hard to keep costs in check, *Talk* was a very expensive magazine to produce. Because of the stratospheric level of hype—goosed by an amazing first-issue interview in which Hillary Clinton spoke publicly for the first time about her husband's infidelities—an expectation was set that nothing short of a spectacular issue every single month would satisfy readers. The pressure was on, and the costs of meeting those expectations stayed high, month after month, even as newsstand sales and subscriptions began falling.

Within six months of the launch, we could tell that *Talk* wasn't working out. After the first issue, which was a smashing success, the circulation growth began to stall, and then sink. Newsstand sales were dropping. The response rate to the inserts—those little subscription mailer cards stuck between the magazine's pages—fell quickly, and they're a key barometer of readers' response to a magazine. So far, the advertising pages were improving, but we desperately needed more readers.

At least one person within Hearst, Mark Miller, the executive vice president and general manager of Hearst Magazines, began sounding the alarm right away. Mark is a pure numbers guy who took pains to look at economic indicators from an analytic rather than an emotional angle. He speaks the language of "benchmarks," and from his point of view, *Talk* wasn't meeting them and wasn't likely to. Our experience is that few magazines that get off to a slow start find the traction they need to succeed.

Yet Tina Brown had a history of turning around struggling magazines. Condé Nast's *Vanity Fair* was the perfect example: it was a perpetual underperformer when Tina took it over, and over time she turned it into the most talked-about magazine on the newsstand, with solid circulation and tons of ad pages. If Condé Nast had pulled the plug on *Vanity Fair* before Tina had a chance to work her magic, they'd have missed out on untold riches.

So how do you know when it's time to pull the plug on a project you love? If you shut things down too soon, you could miss out on a big turnaround. If you shut things down too late, you end up throwing money away. It's a tricky question, one that doesn't have a single right answer. But there is one rule I've come to count on:

Make hard decisions sooner rather than later.

Making decisions that affect people's lives isn't easy. As you can imagine, the part of my job I like least is having to fire people, or shut down entire magazines. But I always keep in mind one top executive's response when asked if he regretted a tough decision he'd made. "The only thing I regret," he said, "is that I didn't make it sooner." If a difficult decision seems inevitable, it's best for everyone not to postpone it unnecessarily.

In the years since we shut down *Talk,* Tina Brown has been quoted publicly as saying she believed Hearst and Disney/Miramax pulled out too soon. I understand why she feels that way, as she'd given the magazine absolutely everything she had and was rightfully proud of the editorial product. But I believe we gave *Talk* as much time as we could, given the numbers we were seeing—and the red ink. And after the terrorist attacks of September 11, 2001, when the advertising market suffered a huge downturn, it was even more difficult to see the magazine's future turning any brighter.

We'd had a number of private meetings internally about *Talk,* including some with Harvey. On the day in late January 2002 when we finally decided to close the magazine, the staff was halfway through preparing the next month's issue. As I stood in the magazine's offices, giving the weeping staff members the news, they understandably asked if they could push ahead and produce that one last issue.

It was very tough, but I had to say no. Two more weeks of work meant two more weeks of costs, and besides, with some of the employees in the room already on their cell phones to their friends (and possibly journalists), we knew that news of the closing would spread quickly. The last thing we wanted was to allow the media to have a long public feast—from the first announcement of closing to the final issue—on the demise of what had been such a promising magazine. Did the staff hate me that day? And hate Hearst, Harvey, and Disney? Probably. But, unfortunately, life as an executive is about making tough decisions, not about being popular. We needed to get the bad news out there and be done with it.

I learned many important lessons from the *Talk* episode. For one thing, it's critical to establish rigorous benchmarks for success ahead of time, then evaluate them without emotion as you move along. For another, I vowed that we'd never again get involved in a magazine over which we had so little editorial control. No matter how much faith we had in Tina, we needed to have some say over what went into the magazine, rather than being the equivalent of bankers for it. And never again would we come in so late in the development stages of a new magazine without restructuring a deal that was fair to all parties.

Finally, the hype we'd been seduced by ended up getting in the way. As Tina Brown herself said in a 2003 interview, "Buzz can be harmful. It certainly was in *Talk*'s case. I mean, we gave an insanely huge launch party that really subscribed to [the movie and theater producer David Brown's] theory of show business—which is 'Never give a party that's better than the movie.' " I'm sure none of us will ever forget that dazzling launch party—but, more important, we have to make sure we never forget its lesson.

BLACK & WHITE

The Devil Is in the Details

Our experience with *Talk* brought home the fact that attention to detail often marks the difference between success and failure. And that's true not only for planning and executing big projects, but in just about every facet of your working life.

The first time I was invited to join the board of a nonprofit organization, I was delighted. Being asked to serve on a board is a sign of respect for your skills and ideas. So I quickly accepted, and when the day of my first board meeting arrived, I walked into the meeting room with a big smile and high energy. Halfway into the agenda, I lobbed what I thought was a great idea into the mix. But to my surprise, the faces around the table looked blank. A short, unenthusiastic discussion ensued, and my idea was quickly voted down. I wasn't crushed, but it was certainly disappointing.

The next morning a fellow board member whom I'd met but didn't know well called and invited me to breakfast. After we exchanged pleasantries, she leaned across the table and asked, "Cathie, have you ever been on a board before?"

"No," I answered brightly. "This is my first."

"Well," she said, "I'm going to tell you how to serve on a board."

I wasn't sure what she meant. I knew what was generally expected of board members: to help guide the organization, provide financial oversight, maintain accountability, that kind of thing. What more was there to know?

"The idea you presented yesterday was great," she told me. "But you should have built support for it in advance. You need to call around, get opinions, and make sure you have a few people on your side before the meeting starts. That way, when you present your idea, you'll already have the seed of collective support."

The minute the words were out of her mouth, the idea seemed so obvious. Yet it had never occurred to me before that *seeding a meeting* was a necessary strategy. As I quickly realized, it's a strategy that applies not just to board meetings, but to any meeting where you plan to present an idea or proposal. If you're trying to win support, why not give yourself a head start?

Seeding a meeting is one of many attention-to-detail strategies that, used wisely, can vault you beyond being good at your job to being great at it. Let's take a look at a few more:

MEETINGS

1. **Keep 'em small, and keep 'em few.**

Ever notice how the more people there are in a meeting, the less gets done? When you have to deal with eight people's opinions, interjections, and body language, the number of useless interruptions grows exponentially. Keep your meetings small—no more than three or four of the most essential people. And for that matter, call a meeting only when you really need one. Don't fall prey to meeting-itis, the disease where every small decision becomes the occasion for reserving a conference room and heating up the coffeepots.

2.   Keep 'em short, and end 'em on time.

Once people get into meetings, they never seem to want out of them. Be sure to start on time—maybe even a few minutes early—and end on the timetable you promised. Also, always go into a meeting with a clear idea of why you're there, and once the purpose of the meeting has been fulfilled, make a break for it! Otherwise it's too easy to get caught up in irrelevant chatter and needless digressions.

3.   Focus on the goal, not on the process.

The first thing I do in every meeting is ask, "What do we want to accomplish here? What decisions are to be made?" Meetings can be for either discussion or decisions—just make sure you identify which one at the outset. Too often, people become enamored of the process, wanting to debate every little detail and explore every hidden avenue, regardless of whether the goal of the meeting is ever reached. Don't get caught up in *process* at the expense of *progress.* It's a good idea to make an agenda and stick to it, putting the most important items at the top, because inevitably those are the ones you'll spend more time on.

4.   Identify the next steps before the meeting ends.

It's a huge time-waster for people to leave a meeting and then engage in multiple emails and phone calls to figure out what needs to be done next. At the end of every meeting, decide right there, while you're all together, what the next steps are. Then designate one person to email everyone with a brief recap of the meeting, the decisions that were made, and action steps. That way there's a written record, and any possible misunderstandings will be resolved quickly.

SEATING

1.   Think before you sit.

When you walk into a meeting room, luncheon, or other work environment, think twice before plopping yourself down in the nearest chair. First, consider what you can gain from a strategically chosen seat, and how you will be perceived, depending on where you sit. If I walk into a conference room where the only two women attendees are sitting together at one end, for example, I sit somewhere else; otherwise it looks too much like the women are huddling together. And at a long conference table, I always avoid sitting at the "black hole" of the corners, where you can't see or be seen by your fellow attendees.

2.   Make your dinner plans carefully.

The first few times I went to conferences, I didn't make my dinner plans very well, ending up dining with either colleagues or competitors—and even, once or twice, giving up and getting room service, which is completely antithetical to why you go to a conference in the first place. Now I make a point of identifying a client or potential client to ask to dinner and making plans in advance. Why not use your time to get some business done, even if it's in a more casual environment?

3.   Leave nothing to chance when you're seating others.

If you're in charge of an event, meeting, or dinner, put serious thought into the seating arrangements. Al Neuharth always did this religiously; he knew who he wanted at his side, and who he wanted to relegate to Siberia. Similarly, when you're in charge of seating for an event, don't think of where people might *like* to sit; think about the most productive possible seating arrangement.

For a large event, I often spend hours just planning the seating—and it always pays off.

RECEPTIONS

1.   Avoid your friends.

Whenever I'm at a business reception or party, I don't spend a lot of time mingling with my friends or close colleagues. Instead, I seek out people I haven't met yet, or those I don't know well. It's a perfect opportunity to make or strengthen connections. In fact, I really look forward to these chances to meet and mingle in a relaxed setting, as it's a convenient and fun way to get to know people.

2.   Know who people are—and let them know who you are.

Before a reception or outside meeting, make a point of learning who will be there and what their titles are. People like to be called by name, and they're flattered if you know who they are before they even tell you. Also, bring business cards, and introduce yourself with both first and last name. And if you'e organizing an event, always use name tags.

3.   Worm your way in.

A few years ago I was taking my then-preteen daughter Alison and her friend to a movie premiere when she mentioned she really wanted to meet the star. I figured she'd be a little shy about it, so I told her she'd need to be a little pushy and worm her way into the group of people that would inevitably surround the star. The same is true for you if there's someone you want to meet—famous or not—at a reception. Even if that person is surrounded, seize your moment! Go up and introduce yourself, because if you decide to wait for a less busy moment, it might never come. So—go, go, go.

4.   Follow up fast.

If you've just met someone at an event or reception, especially if they're well known or powerful, the truth is they probably won't remember you for long. So follow up right away—within twenty-four hours is best—with a quick email, note, or phone call. Don't wait until you actually want to approach them about something specific; the longer you wait, the greater the chance that they'll have completely forgotten you. Ask if you can get together as a follow-up, and be persistent—it might take months to get on the calendar of a particularly busy executive.

PRESENTATIONS

1.   Make sure your AV is A-OK.

Pretty basic, right? Yet you wouldn't believe the number of times I've been in presentations where the person's PowerPoint went on the fritz, or the Internet connection didn't work, or the microphone was dead—whatever mishap you can think of, I've seen it all. And believe me, it's never an impressive sight. Anytime and every time you're scheduled to give a presentation, arrive early, before others are in the room, and double-check your audiovisual equipment. And make sure you know whom to call when trouble arises—get their extension or cell phone number in advance.

2.   Hold on to your handouts.

Whenever you bring handouts to a meeting, remember not to hand them out until you're ready for people to look at them.

As soon as they're in your audience's hands, they'll stop paying attention to whatever you're saying and pore over those handouts as though they contained secret messages from heaven. Control your audience's attention—hold on to those handouts.

3.   Leave the entourage at home.

When we started planning our magazine pitch to Oprah Winfrey's team, one of the first decisions we had to make was who would go to Chicago for the big meeting. Ellen Levine was an obvious choice, because she already had a relationship with Oprah. And as the president of Hearst Magazines, I was the one who'd be making the pitch. After some thought, I decided that two were enough—it didn't make sense to go busting into Harpo's offices with a whole contingent of people. It was a meeting, not a war, so there was no need to show strength in numbers. Similarly, if you've been invited to make a presentation to a potential client, don't come in with a whole gang of people—keep it to two or three. As with in-house meetings, keeping it small will cut back on complications.

OFFICE PARTIES

1.   Greet people at the door.

Standing by the door is a great place to be at a party, especially if you're the host or the boss. Why? Because it's the one place you're absolutely guaranteed to see everyone. Mingling is fun, but the door is the place to be, at least in the beginning, especially if it's important for you to see everyone. At our annual employee holiday party, I position myself at the door fifteen minutes before the start, and stand there until I've shaken all 1,200 people's hands. They like the personal touch, and I do, too.

2.   Leave before it gets messy.

Rupert Murdoch, of all people, gave me this advice: Don't stay too long at the party. If you're the boss, this advice especially applies—because the truth is your employees will be able to loosen up and have more fun once you've left. And even if you're not the boss, remember that there's no benefit to staying to turn out the lights and scrub down the bar. No matter what your position in your company, you're better off not being witness to whatever goes on when the last hard-partying people are on the dance floor or at the bar. Leave while it's still fun—you'll never have cause to regret it.

3.   Don't get drunk.

The annals of office-party history are filled with tales of woe and embarrassment, none of which I will recount here, in the interest of good taste. I'm sure you've heard some classic cautionary tales, too—just don't become one yourself.

TRAVELING

1.   Stay at least a room apart.

In chapter 3, I told the story of how I learned that colleagues really shouldn't have to share rooms if at all possible. Here's the corollary: When you book separate rooms for everyone, try to make them *really* separate, with at least one other room between each one. The truth is, you don't know what your colleagues will be doing during their free time on business trips. And sometimes you don't *want* to know.

2.   Play it safe.

It pays to be cautious as a single woman traveler, even in a business environment. If you're booked in a room at the end of a long hallway, for example, ask for another room to avoid being in an isolated area. And if a male colleague asks to walk you to your room, decline politely, since even though most such requests are completely innocent, you don't need the headache of dealing with the few that aren't. Early in my career I made the mistake of accepting what I thought was a gentlemanly offer of a friendly walk back to my room. While nothing terrible ultimately happened, I'll never forget the image of the guy holding his foot in the door to my room, keeping it ajar while I was trying to close it without breaking his foot. It was an awkward and embarrassing situation—one I made sure I never found myself in again.

3.   Check in early, before you go to your event.

Recently my colleague Michael Clinton and I flew to Chicago for business meetings. We'd booked our rooms at the Ritz Carlton well in advance, but because our schedule was tight, we went straight to the dinner instead of checking in at the hotel first. Mistake! When we made our way to the hotel at 10:30 p.m., after a reception and dinner, we were told our "guaranteed rooms" had been filled. We made a fuss, but the hotel staff said they were completely sold out, and that all they could to was to call another hotel for us. So off we went with our bags into the night, tired and frustrated when we could have been asleep.

HIRING

1.   Don't fall in love with your candidate.

When someone comes in for an interview, know in advance what information you need to get, because some candidates will sweep you off your feet. It's easy to get caught up in a person's charm, but charm doesn't necessarily produce results. So come in with a checklist of the hard questions, and make sure you get answers to them all.

2.   Follow the "three-meeting" rule.

For really important hires, try to meet the candidate three times, at least once at a meal. At the first meeting, you're both selling, which makes it hard to find out what you really need to know. The second time, you can assess important factors, like "Can this person maintain a conversation? Is she interesting? Smart? Pleasant?" By the third time, the conversation is more real, and you can finally assess whether the person has the skills, attributes, and experience for the job.

3.   Mix and match.

Conventional wisdom says you should choose the candidate with the best skills and the personality most compatible with yours. But that's only half of it. Rather than hiring the person you like the best, think about how he or she will fit in with the rest of the team. If your current team is strong in analytical thinkers, perhaps adding a more creative thinker to the mix will juice things up. Also, though hiring a whole team full of younger versions of yourself might feel comfortable, it won't be the best team you could hire. Hire to your weaknesses, not to your strengths.

4.   Go with your gut.

The most important time in any interview is the first five minutes. During that time I can tell many things about a candidate. How does she carry herself? Does she look me in the eye when she speaks? Does she express herself with confidence? You want a candidate who looks great on paper, of course, but you should trust your gut feeling just as much. If you're feeling uncertain about someone but don't know why, believe me—the answer will come out sooner or later. It's best to trust your instincts from the beginning.

FIRING

1.   Do it quickly!

The first time I ever fired someone was at *Ms.* magazine. Valerie Salembier and I went together to do the deed, and the woman was shocked and upset. She launched into a long explanation of why we should give her another chance, and unfortunately we listened and responded. Back and forth we went, for nearly an hour, before we finally realized this woman would keep us there until we either gave her another chance or cut off the conversation once and for all. By the end, Valerie and I were wrecks—and for no reason, as the end result was exactly the same as if we'd done it quickly. From that moment on, I knew that whenever I fired someone, I had to do it quickly and not get sucked into a debate. The reality is, once the words "We're letting you go" are out of your mouth, the person's not hearing anything you say after that anyway.

2.   Pick a neutral spot, and bring someone else.

When you're firing someone, take them into a conference room or other neutral spot. It's tempting to do it in your office, but you can't get up and leave when the conversation is over, and they might try to keep you there a long time. And always have one other person in the room as a witness. In these litigious times, it's best to protect yourself from any potential he-said-she-said situations.

3.   Treat people fairly.

When you fire someone, they're going to feel terrible, so there's no need to rub it in. Even if the person has done something very wrong, and is about to be escorted out of the building, and even if they've been driving you crazy for the last six months and you can't wait to get rid of them, deliver the news firmly but fairly. We've actually had people send notes after getting fired, saying, "Thank you for being so fair and straightforward about it." There's never a downside to taking the high road.

4.   If you're the one being fired, try to take the news as calmly as you can.

Blowing up or getting upset won't help matters, and it can burn bridges that you might need later. Feel free to ask questions, but don't try to change your employer's mind, as the decision has already been made. Most important, try to learn what you can from the situation, to avoid having it happen again.

5.   Don't be afraid to break the mold.

Just like everything else in the workplace, hirings, firings, and other personnel issues don't have to go according to the usual script. Martha Nelson, the longtime editor and now editorial director of *People* magazine, once told me her strategy for moving someone out of a position without actually firing her. "I never really fired anyone," she said. "What I did was bring somebody in with the exact same title. Eventually the incumbent would realize they were being replaced, and move on of their own accord."

And Pat Carbine, in her inimitable way, tells this story about how she once kept an employee who wanted to leave. A woman working for her had made a mistake, and she was embarrassed and deflated. She wanted not only to quit her job, but to leave New York altogether and go back home.

As Pat puts it, "I was listening attentively, and suddenly I had an epiphany. I told her, 'Listen, here's the thing that's so interesting about resignations. For reasons that seem absolutely right and reasonable, an individual might decide they want to resign. But that's only half of it. The other half is that the person on the other side of the desk has to accept it. And I'm not going to do that today. I'm not convinced you're resigning for the right reasons.'" The woman was stunned, but she took Pat's comments to heart. She ended up staying on at *Ms.*, which was good for her and good for the magazine. But if Pat had been afraid to break the mold, she would have been gone.

There's one other very interesting thing about that story. It's a perfect example of Pat's innate ability to gauge people's motivations and needs—a valuable quality that made Pat an exceptional boss. Understanding other people's passions is one key to being a great leader. And as we'll see in the next chapter, understanding your own passions is the key to leading a fulfilled, productive, and satisfying life, both in and out of the workplace.

Chapter 6

Passion

If there's such a thing as a "sales gene," I was definitely born with it. From the time I was a little girl growing up in Chicago, I loved persuading people to buy what I had to sell. First it was lemonade. Then, to what was probably the chagrin of my whole neighborhood, when I was about eight I started going door to door to peddle a small Catholic newspaper. I was so excited and persistent that I even managed to sell subscriptions to a couple of our Protestant neighbors before my parents reined me in.

My father worked in the private-label food business, and my mother was a traditional stay-at-home mom, raising my sister, brother, and me. Dad's company had a manufacturing plant about a ninety-minute drive south of Chicago, where they made gourmet-type mustards, mayonnaises, and salad dressings, and I loved going there whenever he'd take me. Mayonnaise might not be the most dazzling product in the world, but the whole prospect of making a business out of it seemed like magic to me. When I'd see him coming and going from trips, suitcase in hand,

I'd dream about what kind of adventures he must be having on the road.

Thanks to my dad's success at work, our family enjoyed a comfortable middle-class life. I didn't need to work summers while in high school, but I did anyway, because I wanted to. I liked getting dressed up, catching the train to go to downtown Chicago, and walking into an office building or department store. It never felt like *work* to me; it just felt like the coolest, most fun way to spend the summer. Also, I liked earning my own money.

My father worked hard, and he kept on working even after a degenerative eye disease began robbing him of his eyesight while I was in my teens. He had several corneal transplants, none of which was successful, but he never gave up hope. Even when he went completely blind, in his early fifties, he never used a cane and he refused to slow his pace. He wore dark sunglasses, hired a driver to take him wherever he needed to go and an assistant to read to him, and kept on doing just about everything he'd done before.

I like to think I'm similar to my dad in certain ways—our shared passion for business, drive to succeed, and persistence. And I'd like to think that if I ever faced the kind of adversity he did, I'd respond with a real dedication to overcoming it. My father truly was an inspiration to me, in so many ways.

I'm telling you all this because these facts form the roots of whatever success I've had, in business and in life. When I look back at my childhood, high school, and college years, it's amazing how clearly I can trace the interests and inclinations that later shaped my professional life. From those first experiences selling newspapers, to feeling a rush of excitement when I took my first summer job as a cashier and gift wrapper at Marshall Field's department store, I knew what gave me energy and what I liked doing.

If you plan on working forty-hour weeks from age twenty to sixty-five, you'll spend about 90,000 hours of your life at your job. For that reason alone, you owe it to yourself to figure out something you really enjoy doing. And besides, if you're doing something you enjoy, you'll be better at it. Why spend your work life slogging through tasks you dislike when there are so many options to explore? Whether you're just starting out, gaining experience, or contemplating a mid-career change, it makes sense to step back and examine what you're doing and why you're doing it. That might seem very basic, but sometimes it's hard to assess honestly what your feelings are toward your work life. Do you ever

- wonder whether your skills would be more useful in another line of work?

- wake up in the morning dreading the start of the workday?

- find your mind wandering frequently to "what if" scenarios, wondering how your life might have been different if you'd chosen another path?

- suspect you'd be happier elsewhere, but ignore the feeling, as it would just be too difficult to "start over"?

If so, you're certainly not alone. But you're not stuck, either, because at any moment you have the power to reassess your life. In fact, let's use this chapter to do it, right now. One essential starting point is to

> **Be who you are in whatever you do.**

Who was your favorite teacher in high school? If you're like most people, the memory of that person brings an instant smile to your face, as you recall meaningful moments in his or her classroom. And, more often than not, our favorite teachers are the ones who led us into the subjects we ultimately pursued.

Now take a moment to think of your least favorite teachers. I don't know about you, but in my case they were the ones who seemed to be on automatic pilot, teaching out of a sense of duty rather than joy, and just counting the months or years until retirement. These teachers lacked authenticity in their work, which wasn't fair to their students or themselves.

How do you find that authenticity for yourself? It's vital to know yourself, and to act on that knowledge. Here are a few basic questions to get you started:

- Are you an introvert or an extrovert?

- Do you feel more drawn to the corporate world, nonprofits, academia, or something else entirely?

- Would you be happier in a big, established company or at a seat-of-your-pants startup?

- Should you go for an MBA? Or is it better to focus on getting more experience in the working world?

Let's break them down one by one:

1. Are you an introvert or an extrovert?

A long time ago, I took a diversity training course run by a fabulous instructor. She had a lot of great insights, one of which has stuck with me all these years. "Some people recharge their batteries by being quiet and reflective," she said, "while others get their energy from being around others. This is the difference between introverts and extroverts."

Having read more than half of this book, can you guess which one I am? There's no contest—I'm an extrovert through and through. I love being around people, which made the world of sales a natural choice for me. I wouldn't do nearly as well in a job that required me to work alone, and I can't imagine I'd be happy doing it. On the other hand, for those of you who draw energy from solitude, my job probably sounds like torture. Figuring out your answer to this question is a key step for figuring out what kind of work will be most satisfying for you.

As an aside, it's a good idea to take the Myers-Briggs Type Indicator, a tool for assessing your personality traits. The test, which is essentially a questionnaire, provides a quick summary of your personality type—for example, whether you tend to make decisions based on logic or on feeling. Many companies and organizations use this test when hiring at the executive level, the better to choose teams whose skills are complementary. The first time I took it, it revealed insights about my personality that I hadn't ever considered before. So have a look on the Internet for more information, and give it a go. You might learn something new and valuable about yourself.

2. Do you feel more drawn to the corporate world, nonprofits, academia, or something else entirely?

For some people, this question has an easy answer. If you've always wanted to be a chef, for example, you're never going to be happy in an office. But sometimes it's not so clear where your true preferences lie. Working in a nonprofit—a museum, charity, or foundation—can be extremely rewarding, but it may not offer all the benefits of a corporate job, particularly in terms of compensation. Conversely, working in a company can be challenging and remunerative, while perhaps not offering deep personal satisfaction.

And there are layers within these options, too. In the course of my career, I've been offered a number of opportunities to work outside the media world. But while I was flattered and intrigued by the offers, I always came back to the same questions: Will I fit in here? Will I be happy? Will I be successful? Once, during the late-nineties boom years, I was offered a big job at an Internet startup in Silicon Valley. It would have been an exciting and potentially lucrative new field for me, but as I walked around the company's offices, looking at the rows and rows of people silently tapping away at their computers, I just kept thinking, "I'm such a fish out of water here. What in the world do I bring to this party?"

Compare that to my first day at Hearst, when then-CEO Frank Bennack introduced me to twenty or thirty executives in the boardroom. I recognized almost everyone in the room, whether I'd actually met them or not, because I'd been in the media business so long. I knew I wanted everything the job had to offer: to head up a large corporate division, to be back in New York, to be a part of a high-profile media company. Looking around that room, I had a big smile on my face, because it felt like I was at home, in a place where I could make a significant contribution. It's a great feeling—one that you deserve to have in your working life, too.

So how can you determine where you'll be most satisfied? First, do some research. Every company has a website, so go on-line and study its mission, its products, and its services. Many companies also post job openings on their websites, so keep checking back if there's a particular company you really want to work for. And if you really want to find out what it's like to work somewhere, the easiest way is to ask someone who already works there. Taking advantage of your contacts, ask around until you find someone who works there. Most people like to talk about their jobs and their company, so don't be afraid to make that connection.

Second, if you want more substantive experience in a field that interests you—especially if it's in the nonprofit sector—you can always volunteer or intern to get your foot in the door. If you're interested in radio, volunteer at your local NPR affiliate. If you love art, you can work as a docent or guide for your town's museum. Very often these types of organizations are under-staffed, and they welcome smart, motivated volunteer help. And sometimes internships can turn into permanent positions.

Third, give serious thought to how much intensity you want, or can handle, at work. Different industries come with very different schedules, so make an informed choice. If you're interested in investment banking, financial consulting, or working as an associate for a big law firm, are you ready for their hellish hours and demanding deadlines? Or would you prefer a lower-key work environment, where you can wrap up by 5:00 or 6:00 p.m. each day? Either choice has its pluses and minuses; the key is to understand your own personal desires and motivations and make your choice accordingly.

Finally, trust your instincts when you're considering what kind of career you'd like to pursue. Very often your gut will tell you when you're making a false step, even when your brain is telling you otherwise. This is especially helpful if you're being pressured to follow a certain path by your parents, spouse, or colleagues. Don't abandon logic—but do pay attention to what your gut is telling you.

3. Would you be happier in a big, established company or at a seat-of-your-pants startup?

I love startups. I love the adrenaline rush of taking part in a risky new venture, the wide-open sensation that we're making up the rules as we go along. I love the fact that in a startup, you almost always can take part in decisions and projects across the board, rather than being shunted into a specific area within the rigid hierarchy of an established company.

That said, there are real hardships to working in a startup. Uncertainty is one—you never know if your company will survive, much less thrive. It can be frustrating never to know what new issue you might face when you come to work each morning. And you won't have the support you'd have in a larger company; there's no Department of X, Y, or Z to step in and help you with tasks you're having trouble with. So startups are clearly not for everyone.

I'm frequently asked to give speeches to students and interns, and often someone will ask whether I recommend working at a startup company. The answer is a qualified yes. I've worked in four different startups during my career, and I wouldn't trade the experience for anything. If you have a pioneer spirit and can take the pace, the heat, and the uncertainty, then go for it. You'll get an education that you can't get anywhere else. But if you know you need more structure at work, then there's no point making yourself miserable just for the sake of experience.

4.   Should you go for an MBA? Or is it better to focus on getting more experience in the working world?

Ah, the eternal question! Do you need an MBA? And if so, when should you get it? Does it make sense to interrupt your career momentum to go back to school? I faced all these questions early in my career and fortunately had someone to walk me through a foolproof system for making my decision.

It happened when Francis Ford Coppola's startup magazine, which I'd moved to San Francisco to work for, went out of business. At age thirty, I found myself out of a job, out of the New York magazine world, and uncertain what my next step should be. As I've detailed in earlier chapters, I had weaknesses that I knew could hinder my progress as a magazine executive. I wanted to have a more solid understanding of the financial side, and a better grasp of numbers and data. Also, having the credential of an MBA degree would help me get better jobs moving forward, especially since I'd gotten my bachelor's degree from a small college. But was this the time to do it? I went back and forth, trying to decide, and eventually asked a friend who was a New York magazine consultant what he thought.

"There are two reasons to go for an MBA in mid-career," he told me. "First, if you want to make a career change—like moving from publishing into banking—then it's very important." I didn't want to change careers, so that was out. "The other reason," he went on, "is if you've hit a wall with regard to your compensation. If either reason applies, go for it. If not, you're better off continuing to work, because of the income you'll lose and the cost of MBA tuition." For me, the second reason didn't apply either, so I ultimately decided not to do it. And I've been grateful to my friend ever since for having offered a clear test for making my decision.

But what if you're just starting out and haven't established a career yet? I can tell you that if I were just graduating from college now, I would definitely get an MBA. Yes, you can succeed without one, but you'll give yourself a head start by getting one. The base of knowledge you'll receive—including specialized instruction on your weaker skills—will be helpful. Having an MBA on your résumé will automatically vault you into more serious consideration for jobs. And you'll almost certainly feel more confident in the job market for having it, which is a tremendous help.

WHEN I first came to New York and began interviewing for jobs, I felt almost giddy with possibility. Apart from that one awkward moment in the Condé Nast elevator, where I felt like a

hayseed in my conservative Midwestern suit, I always loved going to new offices, meeting new people, and exploring the New
York media world. Looking back, I must have seemed like an
excitable puppy to the executives who interviewed me.

In fact, all that energy worked in my favor at least once. After
interviewing at *Holiday* magazine, I came bounding out to the elevator bank, where a handsome older guy (he was probably all of
forty, which seemed old to me at the time) was waiting for an elevator. "Hello," he said. "I don't recognize you—are you new here?"

"Oh," I answered, "I don't work here—I just had a job interview with Phyllis Tillinghast. It went really well! She seems great,
and of course I love the magazine . . ." and on and on I went, to
the guy's apparent bemusement. After riding down in the elevator, he went his way and I went mine, and I didn't think about
the conversation again—until after I'd been offered the job.
Then my new boss, Phyllis, told me that Elevator Guy had called
her the very next morning to say, "I don't know who that girl is,
but you better hire her, because she is very enthusiastic about
this job." It turned out he was the publisher of the magazine.

This takes us right to our next rule of thumb:

> **Find something that excites you.**

Every job involves doing some things you'd rather not do.
Yet you should be able to find a profession that you enjoy on
its most basic level and, more important, gives you satisfaction.
Otherwise you're not only cheating yourself, but in all likelihood
you're cheating your employer, too.

Someone once asked me, "Don't you ever just want to get
away from magazines for a while? When you go on vacation, do
you run past magazine stands so you don't have to think about

them?" The question at first struck me as funny, because I absolutely love magazines and almost never go anywhere without a tote bag full of them—both ours and those of our competitors. Yet the more I thought about it, the more I realized that not all people are fortunate or persistent enough to have found professions they love so much. On the flip side, perhaps they know what they love doing, but haven't figured out a way to turn it into a profession.

Which brings me back to Atoosa Rubenstein. I opened chapter 1 with a story about Atoosa, who at age twenty-six had impressed me with her drive and desire to create a great magazine for teenage girls. She had a vision for what she wanted to do, and she believed in it completely. While the idea for *CosmoGirl* magazine was a very good one, what sold me on it was Atoosa's passion for the project. She knew what she was good at, and with our help, she channeled that energy into a real, workable product.

Atoosa served as the founding editor of *CosmoGirl* for its first four years, and after Hearst purchased *Seventeen*, we moved her over to become editor there—the position she held when I first started working on this book. Now, as I write this, Atoosa has decided to leave Hearst, to follow a new dream. She wants to create her own multiplatform business, focusing on young women through a variety of media.

Atoosa exuded energy and creativity at Hearst, which of course we miss. That said, I'm happy for her that she's pushing herself to pursue a new dream. After all, we gave Atoosa her big break, and she grew up while she was here, so it's gratifying to see her believing enough in herself to take this big risk.

RIGHT about now, some of you are probably thinking, *Sure, Cathie, it's easy to pursue a dream if you know what it is. But* what if you're having trouble figuring out what you really want in work and in life? It might help to start by figuring out what you *don't* want.

It's okay to say "No, thanks."

Some years ago, I had lunch with the head of a very large cosmetics company. I'd known him for years, and we had lunch regularly, so I was a little surprised when he suddenly shifted the tone of the conversation. "Cathie," he said abruptly, "I have a question for you." He paused, as I sat wondering what could be coming. "How would you feel about being president of my company?" he asked.

There's a lot one could say to such a proposition, but unfortunately the only thing that sprang to my mouth was *"What?!"* I was absolutely dumbfounded—I hadn't seen this coming at all, and almost couldn't believe it. He just smiled, waiting for me to respond in a more coherent way, which I finally managed to do.

"I'm a media executive," I told him, "not a cosmetics executive."

"Well, give it some thought," he said. "And then let's talk some more when you've mulled it over."

Mull it over I did. This was a very well-known, hugely successful company, and the offer was both flattering and intriguing. Yet the more I thought about it, the more I realized that magazines, not makeup, made my heart flutter. So the next time we met, I told him, "This is hard to say, but you need someone who lives and breathes cosmetics—who wakes up in the middle of the night and says, 'It's purple! That's the new color for spring!' Honestly, I'm just not that person."

We talked for a while, and I'm not sure I ever convinced him of my reasoning, but he was very gracious about the whole matter. The reality is, if I had taken the job, I probably would have enjoyed many aspects of it. Even so, I've never regretted the decision. For me, having the chance to be a leader in an industry I love outweighs almost all other considerations.

Okay, now that I've spent most of this chapter exhorting you to follow your dream, and to say no when your heart isn't in something, let me throw a curve in here. There's an important corollary to that advice:

> It's okay to say yes for strategic reasons.

After spending more than eight years at *USA Today*, most of them as the newspaper's publisher, I was ready for a change. My time there had been deeply fulfilling, but also exhausting, and there didn't appear to be any higher positions within Gannett, the newspaper's parent company, to which I could aspire. But where should I go next?

I had two strategic goals: to exit gracefully from *USA Today*, and to land a job as president or CEO of a large division of a media company or organization. Though I had spent the first part of my career in magazines, by this time I'd been out of the magazine world for nearly a decade. There wasn't any clear-cut next step for me to take, so I spent some time considering my options—right up to the day a couple of guys from Booz Allen, the management consulting firm, came to see me in my office.

They were doing a study for two newspaper industry trade associations and wanted to ask me some questions. In the course of our conversation, I learned that the associations, which represented more than a thousand newspapers across the country, were probably going to merge and that they were looking for a CEO to head up the whole shebang. "What the new association will need," one of the consultants told me, "is a CEO to help position newspapers in a changing media world. It will need a much more visible CEO than the ones who traditionally run trade associations."

Right away, the wheels in my head started cranking. They wanted someone who'd be comfortable representing newspapers on a variety of stages, from speeches to interviews to appearances before members of Congress. And they needed someone who was intimately familiar with the ins and outs of the newspaper business. So far, so good. Yet even assuming I could get the job, I already knew it wasn't one I'd want to hold forever. This was very different from what I'd been doing, and I wasn't sure I'd enjoy—or even be any good at—lobbying Congress, which would be a big part of the job. What I really wanted was the chance to run a company, and heading up an important, major nonprofit association would put me a step closer to that.

It wasn't my dream job—but it would be a great next-step job. So I went for it.

As soon as I was named CEO of the American Newspaper Publishers Association (later renamed the Newspaper Association of America, or NAA), I immediately faced questions from reporters wondering why an operating executive like me had chosen to head up a trade association. I finessed the answer as best I could, smiling and saying, "It's a great challenge to think about the future of an entire industry, especially with all the new technologies coming in"—a challenge that still faces the industry today. Then I set about doing the best job I could.

I spent almost five years at NAA and learned a tremendous amount. It wasn't the sexiest job of my career, but it was very satisfying. It also helped me become a more well-rounded executive, and solidified my reputation as someone who could run a large organization. In addition, I got to know the NAA chairman quite well, marking the beginning of a wonderful, productive working relationship that continues to this day. That chairman's name? Frank Bennack, who was then the CEO of Hearst and now continues to serve as vice-chairman of the Hearst board. I didn't get my job at Hearst only because of working with Frank at NAA, but it certainly didn't hurt.

So don't be afraid to take steps in your career that are strictly for strategic purposes. Yes, you want to follow your dreams, but sometimes the path to your dreams involves a carefully thought-out detour. In that same vein, here's a piece of advice you might be surprised to hear from me:

> **Don't be afraid to step out altogether, if that's what you truly want.**

In the fall of 2006, Ruth Diem, Hearst's director of human resources, told me she was planning to take early retirement and would leave the company by the end of the year. I couldn't stand the idea of Ruth leaving—she's a talented, empathetic, and dedicated HR executive.

Yet, concerned as I was about how Ruth's departure would affect Hearst, I couldn't help but feel happy for Ruth herself. At fifty-five, she's young, healthy, and energetic, and by taking early retirement she'll have many years to travel, pursue her interests, enjoy her family—whatever she chooses to do. Ruth has always worked hard, so this wasn't an easy decision for her. It takes guts to walk away from a job you're successful at and enjoy. Though I wanted her to stay for selfish reasons, I applauded her life decision and her courage in making it.

Similarly, my niece, Anne, made a decision to change direction in her career. She had worked at a big advertising agency, then decided to get an MBA. Following that, she joined an Internet company—but after a year, and all the work she'd done to get there, Anne decided it wasn't where she wanted to be. She wanted more fulfillment in her work life, so she made a 180-degree turn, into the world of nonprofits. Anne has been at the American Museum of Natural History for four years now, and though she left behind a more lucrative, fast-paced advertising career, she hasn't missed it for a day.

Because I'm a person who gets so much satisfaction from her job, you might think my message to you would be "Work through rough patches and stick with your career no matter what." It's not.

Of course I want people to find satisfaction in their jobs—and I'd like to think this book will help them. But if you give the business world your best shot and ultimately determine that your true happiness lies elsewhere, it's far more important to pursue that happiness than to be miserable for the sake of a career. This can be true on a permanent basis (assuming you have some other source of income and won't go broke), or just a temporary one. Whether you take time off to raise a family, travel, learn to surf, or whatever, it's vital to seek satisfaction in all aspects of your life, not just work.

And with that, we've reached perhaps the most important message in this book: the idea of cultivating what I like to call a 360° Life. Read on to find out what that means.

The 360° Life

During my sophomore year at Trinity College (now Trinity University) in Washington, D.C., I heard about the option of spending a junior year abroad. I could hardly believe what I was hearing—was this really possible? If so, why wouldn't everyone do it? Right away, I began talking to my parents, neither of whom had been to Europe, about spending my junior year in Italy.

Trinity was a very good school, but it was a small, women-only Catholic institution, and I was itching for bigger adventures. (I remember saying to my father, in a petulant moment, "I'm tired of nerds, nuns, and girls!") Suddenly I wanted to spend a year in Europe more than I'd ever wanted anything. My father's main stipulation was that I had to earn full credit while abroad, so I found a program that would allow transfer of my credits back to Trinity. A few months later I found myself on a plane bound for Rome for a year. It seemed like a dream.

When I look back over my life, I can see I've had some truly memorable experiences and exciting times. But nothing compares with that year in Italy. Even now, thinking and writing about it, I can't help but smile— everything was a new adventure, a thrill waiting to be discovered.

I made friends quickly, and we traveled every week-end, piling into cars or even hitchhiking to nearby towns. On holidays we went farther afield: to Paris and London for Thanksgiving, to the Middle East for Christmas, to Spain for Easter. At New Year's, I drank champagne and danced the bunny hop at the Cairo Hilton, then visited the famed Cedars of Lebanon and rode horses along-side the Great Pyramids of Egypt at dawn. And the summer after my program ended, I hitchhiked with my friend Eugenia, a fun, lively girl from Mobile, Alabama, all the way from Rome to Northern Ireland—something we could do safely in that era, though neither of us ever told our parents. To this day we're still great friends.

That year changed my life. From that time on, I was determined to grab everything I could, to taste and experience the world as fully as possible.

A few years later, after I'd graduated from Trinity and was living in my first apartment in New York, I had a difficult conversation with my mother on one of her visits. She had lived a very traditional life, as a house-wife and stay-at-home mother, and she was troubled by the decisions I was making. "Honey," she said, "don't you want to get married? Don't you want to settle down?"

"Mom," I told her, "I don't know yet exactly what I want, but I want to see and experience everything I can—not stay in one place and do the same things every day. I don't know how it will all turn out, but I just want a different kind of life."

She looked as though she'd been slapped in the face. I hadn't meant for my words to seem like a rebuke, but they clearly stung her. It was as if I were rejecting the values she held most dear—even though I *did* want the things she had, and would eventually have them: a husband, children, and my own close-knit family. I just was too excited about all the possibilities of an exciting career to do it on her timetable.

There's a phrase that came into vogue a while back: *having it all.* For a couple of years, magazines, newspapers, and TV were full of stories about super-women who were doing everything: working full-time jobs, raising perfect children, volunteering at their children's schools, and hosting gourmet dinner parties in their spare time. These women were meant to be an inspiration, but instead they ended up making everyone else feel inadequate—and probably having nervous breakdowns themselves within a few years.

As someone who is often perceived as "having it all," let me just say this outright: I hate that phrase. The implication is that every person wants exactly the same thing, which is completely untrue. You don't have to marry the lawyer or doctor, win the U.S. Open in tennis, and become a CEO all in the same year in order to find success and happiness. Having what I call a 360° Life isn't about reaching the top in everything you do, it's about achieving balance. It means creating a fully rounded existence, one that encompasses deep satisfaction with your personal life, work, and family.

I've given you all kinds of advice in the previous chapters, but now we're truly getting to the heart of the matter. If there's one thing you take away from this book, I hope it's this: Blindly striving to have it all is not the answer. And you don't have to work toward having Cathie Black's all, or your colleagues' all, or even your mother's all. No one can define success and personal satisfaction for you except *you.*

> Have *your* all—not anyone else's.

Here's a confession: I was a workaholic in my twenties. I badly wanted not only to achieve, but to overachieve—to go farther, faster, and do more than anyone else. Whatever it took to get ahead in my career, that's what I spent time doing. I was really happy during those years, and honestly don't regret a moment of all that hard work.

Yet today, with a husband of twenty-five years, two teenage children, and a floppy-eared black Lab, I have a keener appreciation for all the nonwork pleasures life can bring. I still work very hard and travel constantly, but when I'm away from work, I'm truly away from it. Even if you're ambitious, it's not a crime to leave at five-thirty on some days. Because the reality is, you're going to be a better, more effective employee if you have a satisfying personal life.

So, how do you define success for yourself? How do you determine not only what you want in your life, but what you can realistically achieve? One way is by looking at these questions from a slightly different angle: Maybe you can have all the things you want—just not all at the same time. In my case, this meant focusing mainly on work in my twenties and thirties and becoming a mother in my forties. That choice wouldn't suit everyone, especially considering the potential age-related complications of getting pregnant after forty, but it has worked well for me. What would work best for you? We'll explore that question in detail in the next section, as we get down to the nitty-gritty of making your own personal choices.

But before that, here are two thoughts to help guide you. The first is an old carnival metaphor: It's not enough just to go for the brass ring—you've got to enjoy the merry-go-round, too. The second is from Oprah Winfrey, and it's one of my favorite lines ever, because it's such perfect advice: Live your best life. Not necessarily the most successful life, and not anyone else's life—but *your* best life.

Now, let's get into the nuts and bolts of how you can do just that. The first great rule of figuring out how to achieve your 360° Life is this:

Face your choices honestly and directly.

Consider these questions:

- Do you have room in your life for a husband or partner, or are you more likely to get ahead if you stay single and work harder? If you have a boyfriend, is he supportive of your goals at work? Will his expectations change once you're married?

- Is having children versus having a career an either-or proposition for you?

- Is part-time work an option, or is the full-time, two-income household the only kind that will allow you to achieve the standard of living you want?

- If you choose to take a couple of years off to raise your young kids, can you deal with the fact that when you return, some colleagues will have leapfrogged over you in the work hierarchy?

When you start making big choices about your life and career, you must be absolutely honest about answers to these types of questions—otherwise you'll only create more trouble for yourself down the road. Let me give you a few examples.

I married my first husband shortly before going to work at *Ms.* magazine. He and I were good together in many ways, but as I began changing—becoming more attuned to the feminist movement, and more confident in myself at work—our relationship began to suffer. He worked in the male bastion of Wall Street, and was from a pretty traditional Irish family, the youngest child of five. After a while we just grew too far apart to keep our marriage together. After we divorced, I remember thinking that I didn't need a husband to achieve success in my career, and that I was perfectly capable of moving ahead on my own.

There was another truth lurking below the surface, though: I really wanted to have someone in my life to share the joys and frustrations with. Sure, I might have been happy on my own. But there's no doubt that since meeting Tom Harvey and marrying him, I've been much happier than I'd ever have been single. Does this mean everyone should get married? Of course not. Many women are more than happy to remain single. Just be sure to be honest with yourself about what you want.

The question I'm asked most often is about balancing work and family. Many years ago a female colleague asked me about going back to work while my children were infants. Tom and I adopted our first child, Duffy, in 1987 while I was working at *USA Today,* and I went back to work four weeks later. We'd hired a full-time nanny, which allowed me to go back so quickly. Should I have taken more time to adjust to being a mother? Of course. But back then, in the craziness of *USA Today*'s early years, and before workplace laws mandated giving new mothers twelve weeks of maternity leave, being out for three months would have been unheard of, maybe even impossible. Women just didn't do that.

"How did you decide to just go back to work?" this colleague asked me. "Did it bother you to leave your child with a nanny?" Her eyes began to well up, and I suddenly realized she wasn't really thinking of my situation, but of her own. "I want to have kids, too," she said, "but the idea of going back to work and leaving them with someone else just tears me up."

"Well," I said gently, "if you're this torn about it, then it seems you've made your decision already. If you can afford not to work, then that's where your heart clearly is."

Some women want nothing more than to stay home with their kids, and some are dying to get back to work. Most of us fall somewhere in the middle. The key is to make the decision that's right for you—no matter what anyone else thinks your right answer should be.

So, let's say you've made the decision that you want both a family and a career. How can you do it all?

Solve the kids-plus-work equation.

As mentioned above, I went back to work within a couple of weeks of adopting our son, Duffy (we adopted our daughter, Alison, four years later). Tom and I both were comfortable with making the decision to have me go back to work full-time. I did bring Duffy with me to a few offsite meetings at *USA Today,* with nanny or mother-in-law in tow, and to his credit, Al Neuharth—who had very progressive ideas about families and work time—encouraged parents to bring their children to work on occasion. But even with these advantages, I remember what a balancing act it was to raise our kids, work long hours, and do so much traveling at the same time.

A huge part of solving the kids-plus-work equation lies in managing expectations. Many people's lives are affected when you decide to have children. Your colleagues have to pick up extra work during your maternity (or paternity) leave, your clients must deal with new people while you're out, your boss needs to figure out how to manage a team that's missing a key person. And you, of course, have to face the reality that your absence might affect your position at the office.

The first critical step for making all these transitions go more smoothly is to set clear expectations for everyone. How long will you be away from work? Can people call you at home if problems arise? Will you be working a few hours a day, a few hours a week, or not at all? Are you available to come into the office in case of emergency?

I was talking with a colleague the other day who told me, "When I had my first child I made the mistake of saying to everyone, 'Sure, call me anytime.' And, boy, did they!" The phone never stopped ringing, so for her second child, her message was different. "I told them, 'I'm available by phone from eight to nine a.m., and from four to five p.m. during the week. That's it.'" Everyone—

including clients outside the office—knew exactly when to call, and when she was planning to return. And they knew what they could expect from her until then, so there were no misunderstandings.

When you return to the office, make sure the ground rules are clear to everyone. If your child is sick, will you expect to be able to go home? Can you alter your work schedule to accommodate your children's needs? Who will assume your duties in your absence? And—just as important—is there some mechanism in place for assuring that single or childless colleagues don't feel like they're unfairly being forced to pick up all the slack? All these considerations need to be hashed out in advance, so that everyone on the team knows where things stand. If your company or organization is big enough to have a human resources department, pay it a visit to find out if there are set guidelines. If not, have a frank talk with your boss.

These are useful strategies for dealing with situations at work. But what about dealing with situations at home, especially if you can't afford full-time help? It's been interesting to note that over the last decade or so, the very notion of family life has been changing. There seem to be more demands than ever on young women in the workplace and greater financial need for both spouses to work, which has in turn led to looser, more flexible arrangements for child care.

Not long ago I was at a reception in Detroit, talking with a client who was the mother of a young child. "I want to introduce you to someone," she told me, gesturing to a female friend. "This is my daughter's other mother." The two women weren't in a relationship together; the second woman was a neighbor who often took care of my client's daughter. In fact, she did so for lots of the neighborhood kids—not for pay, but just to be helpful.

Her "other mother" description reminded me of the title of Hillary Clinton's first book, *It Takes a Village.* The phrase is actually an African proverb, but it resonates more than ever in our fast-paced, twenty-first-century American society. If you can permit yourself emotionally to allow others into your inner circle—friends, grandparents, in-laws, neighbors, and others—you'll find it far easier to navigate the issues of family and work.

Fortunately for younger women, the role of men in home life and child care has changed dramatically over the last couple of decades. Where once the man was largely absent in these responsibilities, many more are taking an active role. I was recently in the Hearst cafeteria when I saw a couple of guys deep in conversation. As I moved closer, I could hear what they were talking about. "Yeah, she woke up around 3:00 a.m., but I gave her the bottle for about fifteen minutes and she fell right back to sleep," one said. "Oh, mine sleeps through the night now," said the other. I had to laugh—this was not a conversation I'd have overheard even five years ago.

Which brings us to another consideration of creating the 360° Life. For those of you who are single but looking for a partner, it pays to consider what kind of person you ultimately want to have in your life. From the very beginning of my relationship with Tom, it was clear that he fully supported and encouraged my work and would take on his share of duties around the house. In fact, as soon as my mother heard I was dating a Catholic lawyer who was a great cook, she told me, "Drag that one to the altar!" And I've always been glad I did, as my life has been so much more full—not just personally, but professionally, too—thanks to that relationship.

So don't be afraid to aspire to everything you want. It *is* possible to have a family and a career, though time and energy are both finite, so you'll have to make choices and, sometimes, sacrifices. Feel free to explore any solutions to the family-plus-work equation—either traditional or not so traditional—that might work for you. And remember, it's not about whether you can do it all, it's about whether you can be happy whatever you're doing.

CHAPTER 7

Attitude

In the weeks after Francis Ford Coppola's magazine folded, *New York* magazine publisher Jack Thomas paid me a visit in San Francisco. I'd worked for *New York* a couple of years before heading out west, so Jack knew me and my track record. He took me out for a very nice dinner, and about halfway through, he said, "Cathie, how would you like to come back and work for us again, as our associate publisher?"

I paused for a moment, wondering if I should say what I was really thinking. As Jack looked expectantly across the table at me, I decided I should.

"Well, Jack," I told him, "this is probably going to sound arrogant, and you may not like hearing it—but the only job I want at *New York* magazine is yours. I want to be the publisher."

He stopped in mid-chew and put down his fork. "Well," he said, "that's interesting." After a moment he collected himself and we went on dining, though I'm not sure he ever regained his appetite. I didn't end up becoming publisher of *New York* then, but within a couple of years I did. In fact, I was the first woman to be named publisher of a major weekly consumer magazine.

When you saw that a chapter of this book was titled "Attitude," you might have expected a lesson on how to behave properly (or even how *not* to have attitude) at work. But this chapter is about something deeper and far more important. It's about how to develop an attitude of healthy expectation for yourself: how to believe you deserve the kind of job, responsibility, salary, benefits—in fact, the kind of life—that you really do deserve.

A lot of people—especially women—work hard and have great skills, but don't understand or have faith in their own worth. Have you ever

- reacted to a positive performance review with gushing gratitude, even though you had worked hard and earned every accolade?

- responded to praise by insisting you hadn't really done anything special?

- stood in the background as others on your team took credit for your work, because you felt funny about putting yourself forward?

These may feel like perfectly natural reactions when they occur, but they'll hinder your progress in the working world. Humility and modesty are valuable personal qualities, certainly, but they won't do much to advance your position in the workplace. If your first response to being praised is to downplay it, you need to ask yourself why. One of the most important skills you can learn is how to

> Value yourself by your aspirations,
> not your limitations.

I didn't start out thinking I wanted to become the president of a magazine company. During the first part of my career, I never really thought that far ahead. Like many women, I viewed my climb up the corporate ladder sequentially, one job after the next—not as a grand, preplanned campaign.

Yet always, even from the very beginning of my career, I wanted and expected each successive job to be the best job I could possibly get at the time. Take my first job at *Holiday* magazine. I had interviewed for several other entry-level positions, at companies like Doubleday, Curtis Publishing, Time Inc., and Condé Nast, but one of the things that drew me to *Holiday* was the fact that my title would be sales assistant rather than secretary. The job responsibilities and salary might have been exactly the same, but I figured I'd get an even better job next time by holding out for a more impressive-sounding title to start with.

It would have been easy for me to think, *You know, I really don't have any particular skills that set me apart from being a secretary, so maybe I should be happy with that.* The reality was, thanks to a few summer jobs in offices, I knew how to type, answer the phone, and file, and that was about it. But instead of agreeing to define myself according to my *limitations,* I chose to value myself according to my *aspirations.* This is a crucial distinction, as it forms the most basic building block for eventual success in your work life.

There's only one person who can truly hold you back in the workplace, and that's you. Sure, some people may try to take credit for your work, thwart your efforts, or otherwise undermine you, but if you refuse to be intimidated—that is, if you maintain an essential confidence in your own talent and contributions—they'll never be more than temporary hindrances. In fact, having confidence in whatever skills you have is often more important than having truly exceptional skills. Let me explain what I mean.

One night at the dinner table, when I was about seven years old, I announced to my parents, "I want to start horseback riding." No one else in my family cared a thing about horses, but I'd been to a nearby stable several times, and I was mesmerized by the horses, the smells, the instructors in their high boots—the whole atmosphere. So I started taking lessons, and though I was never great, I worked hard and really enjoyed doing it.

It never occurred to me that I might not be as good as other girls who'd been riding longer or were more technically proficient. Several years later, one friend who was an excellent rider said to me, "Cathie, I'm a much better rider than you, but somehow, when you're in front of a judge at a horse show, riding around that ring, you just act like you're on top of the world." I hadn't thought about it before, but she was right. I usually looked like a better rider than I actually was because of my bearing. And over time I began to notice that people tend to fit into one of four categories when it comes to their attitude about their own abilities:

- They're good at what they do, and they know it.

- They're good at what they do, but they don't know it or don't believe it.

- They're not very good at what they do, and they know it.

- They're not very good at what they do, but they think they are—or at least present themselves like they are.

In my experience, more women than men fall into the second category. They're good at what they do, and they're incredibly valuable to their teams at work, but for some reason they continually undervalue themselves. Of the four categories, this is not only the most self-defeating but one of the most common. (And by the way, for what it's worth, far more men than women seem to fall into the last category.) So don't make the mistake of undervaluing yourself and your efforts—you'll only succeed in blocking your own progress.

AS I write this chapter, a story in the *New York Times* titled "Gender Pay Gap, Once Narrowing, Is Stuck in Place" is causing quite a stir. According to the article, women's pay levels, which have always been lower than those of men in similar jobs, began to catch up in the 1980s and 1990s. But since then, women with four-year college degrees have seen the gap widen between their salaries and those of their male counterparts. It's a big step backward for the notion of gender equality at work.

In light of that data, it's an unfortunate truth that an employer might not offer you a salary commensurate with what you're worth. But fortunately it's always within your power to ensure you don't accept anything less than what you deserve. So

> Stick to your compensation guns.

From the first time I pressed an employer for a bigger salary (way back at *Holiday* magazine, as described in chapter 2), I've never been shy about asking for the level of compensation I felt I deserved. You can do it too—even if it feels awkward or pushy. It's just a matter of learning to value yourself properly.

The first and best rule to remember is this: your bargaining power is strongest before you accept the job, so negotiate hardest then, when the employer wants to make you an offer. The fact is, the higher you value yourself (without going overboard), the more respect you'll gain from potential employers. If you present yourself as knowing what you deserve—as having an expectation of appropriate compensation for your skills and responsibilities—you'll help your chances immensely. It's simple cause-and-effect: when you show that you respect yourself, others will respect you more.

Admittedly, this isn't always an easy path. You might end up getting push-back from the person doing the hiring, or eventually from others in the company, if you stick to your guns and ask for what believe you deserve. I found this out the hard way when I took the ANPA (later NAA) job I told you about in chapter 6. The experience I had was not only disconcerting but almost surreal.

This was a big, high-profile job, and the organization's board was anxious to hire a well-known industry presence. Frank Bennack, who was the chairman of the search committee, had asked me, "Are you interested in the job?" And I'd told him, "Yes, assuming the compensation is equal to what I make at *USA Today*. I'm not interested in a salary cut."

So I negotiated my contract based on the usual factors: the comparable salary for other heads of big trade associations, my level of experience, and the amount I wanted to make (building on my current compensation at *USA Today*). Because I was moving from a publicly held company (Gannett) to a trade association, they would need to bump up my actual salary to compensate for the stock options I'd be losing. We agreed to terms fairly quickly, and I started work, excited about the challenge of tackling a new position.

A few months later an influential local magazine called the *Washingtonian* ran a story with a picture of me and a provocative headline questioning whether I was really worth the salary I was receiving. Now, admittedly, not a lot of people in Washington made salaries comparable to mine at that time, but other big association heads—men like the late Jack Valenti, the longtime head of the Motion Picture Association of America—certainly did, and no one was questioning them. My husband, Tom, was annoyed by what he saw as the inherent sexism in the question. (He also endured a lot of ribbing from colleagues at the Veterans Administration. "Everybody was faxing the story around, saying, 'Did you see how much Tom's wife makes?!'" he later told me with a laugh. One of the many things I love about Tom is how unconcerned he is about my out-earning him.)

How could I not feel awkward about seeing a headline like that? It felt invasive and embarrassing—and yet not once did I feel it might possibly be right. By any reasonable, objective criteria, I wasn't overpaid. If my salary seemed excessive to others, well, that was their problem. But seeing that magazine story sure didn't feel good. It was also no fun knowing that people at work were whispering about it behind my back.

So stand your ground, but be prepared for push-back. And remember, too, that there's a reason why certain jobs pay really well, or even above the market—they often come with their own diabolical headaches, in the form of crazy hours, Herculean tasks, nightmare bosses, and the like. Get in there and negotiate a salary you'll be happy making. Because once again, as with so many things in life, if you don't do it for yourself, who will?

No less important than negotiating a good salary is negotiating—and taking advantage of—your benefits. That means:

Take the vacation time you deserve.

In my second year at *USA Today*, as the newspaper was fighting to survive and the staff was working 24/7 (before that term was even invented), I decided I had to take more than one week's vacation. I was exhausted. Tom rented us a flat in the south of France for two weeks in August, and although I was certainly

entitled to the vacation, I had to screw up my courage to tell Al
Neuharth I planned to take that much time. No one at Gannett
ever seemed to take a vacation, so I knew he wouldn't be happy,
and I'd have to stand my ground to make sure he didn't manage
to bully me out of it. I decided to give him lots of advance notice
by telling him in early June.

Neuharth was standing next to Charles Overby, his executive
assistant, near his office one morning when I made my move. "Al,"
I said, "I've just sent you a memo, but I want to tell you in person. I'll be in France on vacation the last two weeks of August."

He turned to face me, clearly surprised. "You're *what*?" he
barked. "You're going to France? For *two weeks*?" He didn't actually shout, "Cathie, are you *insane*?" but the sentiment definitely
hung in the air.

I knew I'd never get the vacation I deserved if I didn't stand
up to Neuharth right at this moment. "Yes," I said. "Two weeks.
In France."

He sized me up for a moment, shrugged, and said, "Okay.
Just make sure you're in touch with the office." He then turned
back to Charles Overby. And that was it.

Later, Charles came up to me and said, "Cathie, I can't believe
you did that! I would never have had the courage to ask for *two
weeks*! Did you see his face?" Charles laughed, and went on, "Well,
that broke the ice. Now I'm asking for time off in August, too."

Your benefits, including vacation, are every bit as important
as your salary and title, so don't be afraid to press for what you
need and want. If a medical condition requires you to have a
very comprehensive health plan, ask your employer for what you
need. If you want three weeks' vacation rather than two, then
ask for it (giving your boss plenty of advance notice, of course).
The worst that can happen is that you'll be turned down.

You want to work for an employer who values your skills, so
look at it this way: if a potential employer is turning down rea-

sonable requests, they're probably not someone you want to work for anyway, since that kind of attitude will likely be prevalent throughout the company. Or maybe they simply can't offer what you want; a small startup company, for example, probably won't be able to give you the four weeks' vacation you want. It's up to you whether you make an exception because you really want a particular job.

And for heaven's sake, use the vacation time that you've earned. Too many people let their vacation time pile up, never taking their full amount unless they're about to lose it. Busy as I've ever been at any job, we've always found time to go on family vacations—from a dude ranch to the beach to a safari to Disney World—all of which gives you time to restore yourself, be refreshed, and spend some time with your family. It's another important component of having a 360° Life.

Very often, finding satisfaction at work is simply a matter of creating the conditions for it. When you negotiate the salary you feel you deserve, or when you allow yourself a day or two off to recharge your batteries, you're giving yourself the tools for a more satisfying, and therefore more productive, work life. A good employer will recognize that.

Here's another great way to give yourself the tools to succeed:

Get out there and network.

Networking is another one of those words—like *mentoring* and *power*—that I've never liked, partly because it feels so overused. Yet the idea behind networking is incredibly constructive. Whenever you can take the opportunity to expand your circle of friends and colleagues, you should—and there are numerous organizations, conferences, and gatherings to help you do it.

I've attended all kinds of conferences over the years, rang-
ing from small, informal gatherings to invitation-only events
like *Fortune* magazine's annual Most Powerful Women's Summit,
or the star-studded Allen & Co. media conference in Sun Valley.
Early in my career, I went to conferences with two specific goals
in mind. First, I wanted to meet as many people as I could, for
my own personal and professional growth. Second, I wanted to
make useful business contacts—to meet potential ad sales clients,
or even potential hires. It wasn't just about the bonding experience with other professionals; it was also about seizing business
opportunities where I could find them.

Does that sound calculating? It shouldn't. Of course, it's
helpful for us as professional women to have places to bond with
other women—that's one of the reasons I started our Mind, Body,
Soul conference. But there's no reason not to multitask (another
overused word!) and take the chance to do some business at the
same time.

So, where to begin? If you do a Google search on the words
business, women, and your town's name, you should find several
useful links. Your local newspaper's business section is also likely
to have listings for events and organizations in town, and you
can check with your local chamber of commerce as well. A mentor can help steer you toward a group that will suit your needs,
or you can even start up a group yourself. It's easy enough to put
together small roundtable discussions with other working women,
by email or through notices posted in other offices.

Any kind of networking is useful, but women's networking
can be particularly valuable, because it's not always possible to
penetrate the men's networks that exist. The so-called old boys'
network is not as ironclad and closed to women as it once was,
but it's still alive and well. Despite the progress women have
made in the last couple of decades, men still make up the vast

majority of company CEOs and board members. According to figures released by the nonprofit organization Catalyst, women lead only nine of the five hundred companies that make up the Fortune 500. And just 16 percent of all corporate officers in those companies are women.

A December 2006 article in the *New York Times* offered surprising insights into how far women still need to come to be accepted as peers by men, even when they've already scaled the corporate ladder. The article described the experience of Carol Bartz, an accomplished, longtime CEO in the tech industry. Here's an excerpt from the article:

> Despite her hard-won reputation as an astute business-woman, Ms. Bartz found herself repeatedly skipped over during a recent meeting of business and political leaders in Washington. The reason was that the men at the table assumed that she was an office assistant, not a fellow executive. "Happens all of the time," Ms. Bartz says dryly, recalling the incident. "Sometimes I stand up. Sometimes I just ignore it."

I'm lucky enough to work in an industry with a higher percentage of women in executive roles, so I haven't faced the kinds of attitudes some other women executives do. But if you're interested in more male-dominated fields—for example, investment banking and certain technology fields—you'll need to be ready to face possible bias at work. You might be fortunate enough that it's never an issue, but it's smart to be prepared. So let's have a look at how you can do that.

Be careful not to get a chip on your shoulder.

It's easy to get a chip on your shoulder about someone else's behavior, but ultimately that chip only weighs you down and does nothing to solve the problem. Here's an example of what I mean.

One of my first bosses was a very demanding woman. She had her own way of doing things and expected the rest of us in the office to follow suit, no matter how inconsequential or even silly her requirements. She insisted that we never use paperclips in file folders, that we staple papers at a certain angle, that we keep things on our desks in a certain order. It was borderline obsessive, yet even today I can't see a paperclip in a file folder without reaching to take it out.

When we'd get home from work, my roommates and I would swap stories, and I'd tell them all the details of my boss's latest demands. Months later, when my boss left for another job, one of my roommates said to me, "You must be so relieved! She sounded horrible to work for!"

"She did?" I asked. Even though my boss had made quirky demands on us, she certainly wasn't horrible—in fact I liked her quite a lot. Having quirks like hers came with the territory. Objectively, maybe she *was* a little tough, but the fact that I never focused on that helped me immeasurably in my job, because I didn't spend any energy fretting about it.

Although this wasn't a case of sexism, it illustrates the best way to deal with any minor sexism issues you might encounter at work. Because most issues will in fact be minor ones, the way you respond to them will ultimately be far more important than the issues themselves. Not every throwaway comment by a man is harassment, and not every perceived slight is intended as such. So choose your battles carefully; with common sense and sensitivity, it's usually possible to keep smaller problems from turning into bigger ones. If, however, you are encountering true hostility or real sexual harassment on the job, you have every right to speak up. Get advice from your human resources department first, so you know the best and most effective way to address the problem.

It could be that you feel confident you won't encounter workplace discrimination against women. In the last few years, as I've talked to dozens of young women at Hearst, other young businesswomen, and college students, I've noticed that fewer young women feel as though sexism is a prevalent issue for them. Most say their male colleagues treat them as equals, and they don't think about male-female working relations as an issue.

Harper's Bazaar publisher Valerie Salembier has noticed this trend, too. "Women in their twenties and thirties believe they can do anything," she said to me recently. "They'd never be thankful for their jobs. I spent years being thankful for the jobs I got!"

Her remarks made me think of Gloria Steinem's familiar rant: "Women have a terminal case of gratitude!" she'd say. "If you give us half a loaf of bread, we say, 'Oh, thank you so much!' How come it never occurs to us to say, 'What? Only half a loaf?'" Yet, bit by bit, the "terminal gratitude" Gloria observed seems to be disappearing, and with any luck, glass ceilings and old-boy networks will eventually follow suit.

That said, another comment I hear frequently from young women makes it clear that not every issue has been sorted out: "How can I communicate directly without seeming aggressive or obnoxious?" They wonder whether a strong woman is inevitably perceived as a difficult woman, and whether women have to communicate differently from men to get the same point across. I want to reassure them that

> You can be strong without being obnoxious.

Recently a young woman described how she often talked around what she really needed in an effort not to seem too demanding. She'd started off on the bottom rung at work, but as she moved higher and people began reporting to her, she realized she had no idea how to communicate with them. She didn't want them to think she was lording her new power over them, so she always couched her directives in soft, apologetic language: "I hope you don't mind if I ask you to . . ." or "It would be really helpful if you could maybe . . ."

"At some point," she said in frustration, "you just want to say, '*I need it now!*'" But for some reason she—and many others like her, apparently—felt that saying that directly would come across as aggressive or unfriendly.

As I related in earlier chapters, I used to come across as more aggressive, a trait that some employees at *Ms.*, in particular, found difficult to deal with. After making a conscious effort to lead with greater sensitivity—an effort that continues to this day—I've smoothed out my style. Yet I'm not a softie at work. I'm very direct with employees, and I have no problem making clear when I'm unhappy or want something done differently. And although I do enjoy small talk (and a little gossip) as much as the next person, I don't have much time for it at work, and am quick to steer the conversation back to the agenda so that important matters get attended to. These aren't classically "nice" characteristics, but they haven't negatively impacted my reputation as an executive at all.

The moral is this: It really is possible to be direct without being overbearing. Here are some simple, straightforward tips on how to do it.

1. Focus on being respected rather than on being liked.

It's a natural human instinct to want to be liked, and it can also be quite helpful professionally when the people who work with you like you. Yet it's far more important to be respected, as that's the quality that breeds success in a work environment. Think about the office jokester who always misses deadlines, and you'll understand exactly what I mean. Everyone may love him, but without respect, he's never going to get anywhere.

Keep in mind, too, the crucial difference between being respected and being liked: One is in your control, and the other is not. Some people won't like you no matter how much you try to win them over; it's just a matter of personal chemistry. But if you conduct yourself in a way that commands respect, people will respond to it, even grudgingly. And of course, interestingly enough, when you focus less on whether people like you, they'll tend to like you more.

2. Beware the fine line between humor and sarcasm.

One of the things I've had to work on over the years is recognizing the difference between a funny remark that's just funny, and one that's cutting. Humor is an incredibly valuable asset—a good laugh has a positive effect in the office—but all it takes is one ill-considered remark to set someone on edge and cast a pall on a good working relationship. If you find yourself inclined to make cutting remarks, there's probably some deeper reason behind it, and your colleagues and employees will sense that. Also, it's best to be straightforward about problems or issues you have with people, and save the humor for lighter topics.

3. Don't try to communicate through hints or double meanings.

One of the most frustrating exercises for any employee is trying to discern whether her boss is trying to communicate something through tone, hidden meanings, or hints. There's a control issue here. When you make people do extra work to figure out what you're really saying, you throw them off balance unfairly. Over the years, associates have regularly expressed their appreciation that when I talk to them, what they hear is exactly what I mean. I always try to communicate with people in the simplest, most straightforward way possible. It shows respect for the people you're talking to, leads to fewer misunderstandings, and improves morale in the office.

4.   Trust that your comments will be received in the spirit they are delivered.

A few pages ago I described a young woman who feared that by simply saying "I need it now," bluntly and with no preamble, she would come across as obnoxious or aggressive. "Well," I asked her, "is that what you think when someone speaks that way to you?"

"No," she said. "But somehow it seems different."

The mistake this woman made was in second-guessing other people's responses to her; she just needed to say her piece with confidence, and expect the message to get through. When you're nervous about saying something, the listener will generally assume you have some reason to be nervous about it. If while you're speaking you're thinking, *I hope this doesn't come across as rude,* the chances are far greater that it actually will. If you're going to communicate effectively and gain the respect of your employees and colleagues, you must learn to trust that your comments will be received as you delivered them. That kind of attitude will bring you success far faster than you ever expected.

ONCE, while Al Neuharth was an executive at the Knight newspaper chain, he scheduled a 1:00 p.m. meeting at the office of his boss, Jack Knight. Just as their meeting started, Knight got a phone call. It was the president of Gannett, Paul Miller, calling to inform Knight that Neuharth, who was at that moment sitting a few feet away, would be leaving Knight to take a job with Gannett.

Knight was, not surprisingly, stunned. And he'd probably have been even more stunned if he'd known that Neuharth had orchestrated the whole thing, making sure he'd be sitting right there with Knight when Miller gave him the news. As Neuharth later explained it, he wanted Knight to know that Miller had pursued him, not the other way around. But knowing Neuharth, I suspect there was another reason, too. He knew that arranging for the president of Gannett to make that call on his behalf would make Knight see him as a force to be reckoned with.

I love this story, because it's a perfect example of Neuharth's chutzpah and determination. He never thought twice about giving himself any advantage he could, even if he had to arrange a little ruse here and there to do it. We all could learn a thing or two from Neuharth about how to

---

Orchestrate (and expect) your own success.

The Neuharth story may be an extreme example, but the lesson behind it is good. You should never feel awkward or reluctant about creating advantages for yourself. And if you're working hard and producing results, you have every right to expect the recognition, bonuses, or promotions that will come your way.

Again, this is a skill that men seem to have in greater proportion than women. The story that always reminds me of this involves a man at Hearst who said to me one day, "I've been here for a decade, and *I've* never been named publisher of a magazine!"

He seemed to feel slighted, when of course there are numerous other considerations—not just longevity in the job—that lead to being named publisher of a magazine. It's a tremendously coveted job, the highest business position at a magazine, yet this man seemed surprised it hadn't just been handed to him. It's hard to imagine many women making a similar statement.

One reason some women tend to have lower expectations for themselves can be found in this comment made to me by a young woman at Hearst: "If I suggest an idea and nine people say, 'It's great,' but one person doesn't like it, I get really hung up on that one dissenting vote." Very often, women want the 100 percent buy-in—the absolute certainty that they're correct, deserving, or prepared—before they'll go out on a limb. That is not only unrealistic, but self-defeating. Too often, if you try to please everyone, your message ends up so muddled that you end up pleasing no one.

Finally, the attitude question is not only about learning how to succeed. It's also about learning how to respond to success:

> **Take the credit when it's yours.**

When I was named president of *USA Today*, I started to get a lot of attention and, when things went well, accolades, in the press. There were few women in positions comparable to mine, and that only added to the amount of play the stories got. At one point I said to my husband, Tom, "You know, I'm getting a lot of credit here. But I have a great team behind me, and they're a huge factor in the success we're having. It doesn't seem fair."

"Cathie," he said, "just take the credit when it's yours—because they'll sure as hell give you the blame if it fails." And as the

"Can Cathie Black Save *USA Today*?" headline showed, Tom was right; it was my head that would have been on the block had we failed. So I decided to follow Tom's advice, accepting credit when I deserved it. You can accept praise with humility, but the bottom line is, do accept it. You've earned it.

Cosmopolitan

Sitting at the conference table in the office of Frank Bennack, Hearst's CEO at the time, I thought, *Oh God, Frank is going to have a heart attack right here.* His face was bright red, and the veins were standing out on his neck. In all the time I'd known Frank, I'd never heard him raise his voice, but in this meeting with the new *Cosmopolitan* editor, Bonnie Fuller, he seemed about to blow his top.

Frank had asked Bonnie to present her ideas for *Cosmopolitan,* the magazine that had been edited for the previous thirty years by the legendary Helen Gurley Brown. Helen had turned *Cosmo* into a juggernaut, nearly tripling its circulation from about 900,000 to just under 2.5 million. *Cosmo* was now the top-selling magazine for young women, and Helen—a waiflike, jewel-bedecked force of nature—was the face of it. She'd poured incredible energy into the magazine, showing up at events all over New York and purring her trademark "Hello, pussycat!" greeting to whomever she met.

Cosmopolitan was our biggest earner, so throughout Hearst's corporate floor, there was understandable trepidation about turning over the reins—even to a proven magazine talent like Bonnie Fuller, who had successfully run Hearst's *Marie Claire* for two years before coming to *Cosmo.*

With that in mind, one might have expected Bonnie to tread carefully when she took over the magazine. Instead she came in with guns blazing. She decided to overhaul *Cosmo*'s look, and she brought in her own team to do it. Bonnie had spent the past couple of months hunkered down in a basement office with her team, redesigning the magazine, even as Helen worked on her final issues in the *Cosmo* offices. With the date of Bonnie's first issue approaching, this meeting had been scheduled so that she could show Frank the new look.

As Bonnie confidently showed him the cover and the first thirty pages of the magazine, you could see Frank's face tense up. I had seen the redesign, and it was very different from the current *Cosmo,* with better photography, stronger graphics, and more color. "Bonnie, what have you done?" he asked, his voice rising. "Who did this? Who's on your creative team?"

Bonnie listed several names, including her main collaborator, new creative director Donald Robertson.

His eyes widened. "Well," he said, "what about Helen's staff?"

"They're all leaving," Bonnie replied. "Or they've left."

Frank looked stunned. "You mean to tell me that the people who have produced this unbelievably successful magazine for decades, which has earned hundreds of millions of dollars over the years, are all gone?" he snapped, his face reddening. "Don't you think those people know a little something about producing a magazine that sells?"

I looked at Bonnie. To my amazement, she just sat there coolly, poker-faced, waiting Frank out. His outburst didn't seem to rattle her in the least. He went on for a minute or so, and when it appeared he was waiting for her to answer, she spoke.

"Frank, this is the right decision," she told him calmly. "This is a very visual generation, and we need the magazine to reflect that. It's the right thing for *Cosmopolitan*. Don't worry—it's going to be fine. It's going to be great."

I'm not sure Frank was at all soothed by Bonnie's words that day, but she did go ahead with her redesign. And just as she'd said, it was the right thing to do for the magazine. Helen had done an absolutely fantastic job, but she was a words person in an increasingly visual age, and foolproof though the magazine's formula seemed to be, it did need to be updated for a new generation. Bonnie's instincts for pushing *Cosmo* into a new and different age were right on the money.

There's an excellent lesson in this, one that has since repeated itself at *Cosmo* with Bonnie's successor,

Kate White. No matter how successful your product or project may be, it's important to

> Refresh and reinvent.

Considering the success of *Cosmopolitan* under Helen Gurley Brown, the instinct to leave it alone—the "if it ain't broke, don't fix it" approach—was a natural one. Yet Bonnie understood that the time to push the magazine toward the future was now, not later, when it might seem outdated. Successful as *Cosmo* was, Bonnie wanted to make it even more so. She wanted to play to win, rather than play not to lose.

I wasn't a fan of everything Bonnie did. For one thing, as I wrote in chapter 5, I'm not an advocate of starting a new job by throwing bombs left and right, firing the old team, and leaving the survivors in shock. There was definitely a lot of that in Bonnie's first months. Yet Bonnie's term as editor was a net positive for many reasons, including climbing newsstand sales, the complete redesign, and a terrific tagline, "Fun Fearless Female." The greatest taglines are those that can only apply to one magazine, and this one sums up *Cosmo*— and only *Cosmo*—perfectly.

Which brings us to the key part of any strategy to refresh and reinvent: even as you update and improve a product, you must take care to preserve its essential character—the thing that keeps people coming back to it. In *Cosmo*'s case there are certain basic elements that haven't changed in years, and probably will never change in the next hundred years. Young women will always be looking for advice on relationships, sex, beauty, jobs, shopping, fashion, health, and self-esteem—all the subjects women have had on their minds for generations.

The Coca-Cola company, on whose corporate board I serve, gave the consumer world an example of how far was too far to go in changing a beloved product. In 1985 the company released New Coke, replacing the original drink formula that had endured for decades. Taste tests had shown that people liked the new drink better—but consumers reacted vehemently. They bombarded the company with angry letters and calls, begging for regular Coke to be brought back. Seventy-seven days after New Coke was introduced, the company did just that. It was an expensive and embarrassing misstep, but it was corrected swiftly.

So the trick is to keep up with the times—to explore new product enhancements while knowing which boundaries should be left intact. One editor who's done this very well is Bonnie Fuller's successor at *Cosmopolitan,* Kate White. She's shown a keen instinct for how to

---

Think bigger and broader, brand-wise.

When Bonnie Fuller left *Cosmo* after just two years (she left to become editor at *Glamour,* where she stayed only a slightly longer time), we needed to find a great editor quickly to replace her. I immediately thought of Kate White, who was then editor of *Redbook,* and called her on a Saturday to ask her to meet me on Sunday afternoon. "You're not firing me, are you?" she asked. "Of course not," I told her. "Just meet me in my office at five. I want to talk to you about something important."

Kate arrived promptly, and after a few pleasantries I got right to the point. "How would you like to be editor of *Cosmo*?"

I thought she was going to fall off her chair. "You've got to be kidding!" she said. "Oh, this is fantastic!" She told me later she'd had no idea that was what I wanted to ask her, but as soon as the words were out of my mouth, I could see the gears of Kate's brain start turning. This would be an opportunity for her really to flex her skills on our most important brand. In the nine years since, those gears have never stopped turning—and neither have the profits.

Kate has been a real force for expanding the *Cosmopolitan* brand, including launching a book division, Cosmo Books, which has produced such incredibly successful titles as the *Cosmo Kama Sutra,* which has more than 400,000 copies in print. She also took the initiative on partnering with Sirius satellite radio, creating a specialized channel called Cosmo Radio. The magazine also has Cosmo Mobile, where readers can sign up to get their daily horoscopes and headlines through their wireless phones as well as an extensive website. Kate has done much more than edit the magazine well; she and publisher Donna Kalagian Lagani have turned it into a multiplatform brand powerhouse, which is a lot harder to do than it looks.

Helen, Bonnie, and Kate each put their own stamp on *Cosmopolitan.* They're different kinds of editors, with very different skill sets, and if any of them had tried to be like the others, they wouldn't have brought their own unique improvements to the magazine. There's a great lesson here: Have the courage to push forward, making your product, company, or organization better. And have confidence in your own unique way of doing it, because you'll be bringing something to the table that no one else can.

CHAPTER 8

Leadership

What pops into your head when you hear the word *leader*? If you're like most people, you envision a general leading soldiers into battle, or a politician rousing a crowd to action. The word leadership usually calls to mind proactive, forceful action.

Yet there are more-subtle aspects to being a great leader. And though they may be less obvious, they're every bit as important, especially for those who don't possess the natural power and charisma of a "born leader." It took me an entire career to learn these secrets of great leadership, so I want to give you a jump-start by singling out the essential ones here. First:

> Lead with affection (but don't call it that at the office).

At the Mind, Body, Soul conference a few years ago, an advertising executive named Mary opened up to the group with a story about her boss. Mary had steadily ascended the corporate ladder over the years, working long hours and pushing herself relentlessly in an effort to get to the next level. But when she made it to the top rung, as president of an ad agency, she began to fall apart.

She found that as the top executive, she wasn't doing the same kind of work she'd done on her way up—work she loved and was good at. She wasn't meeting with clients and pitching new business nearly as much anymore; instead, she was managing others who were doing so. She was also spending more time on administrative tasks, such as budgets, personnel matters, and financial reviews. And suddenly she realized she wasn't as good at her new tasks. Mary became increasingly unhappy in her job, and began not only sleeping less but having one glass of wine too many. So she went to the chairman of her parent company and said, "I need to take a leave of absence. I want four weeks off."

If you were the chairman, what would you do in a situation like this? He had several options available:

- Let Mary take the four weeks off—she'd been working hard and needed to pull herself together.

- Let Mary take the four weeks off, but ask her to be available for important meetings or phone calls. After all, how would it look for the agency president to be completely out of the loop?

- Ask Mary to take a shorter period off and then assess whether she needed more time.

- Fire Mary. If she couldn't take the pressure, she shouldn't be president of the agency.

He chose none of those options. Instead, he said to her, "Mary, four weeks isn't enough. You really need some time to think about your life and assess your priorities. Take more time—take two months."

Mary was stunned. She had never imagined he'd be so supportive. Feeling guilty, she said, "Well, of course I'll be here for next Thursday's business meeting—and I can come in for really important presentations during my time off." But the chairman said, "No. A leave of absence is a leave of absence. I don't want one phone call from you for the next two months. When you leave tonight, that's it. Leave your Rolodex, your cell phone, and your BlackBerry right here."

Sounds too incredible to be true, doesn't it? As Mary was telling her story, we all sat riveted by this unusual tale of corporate kindness. And Mary did take the whole two months off. She took long walks, went to museums, and read books, all of which served to refresh her outlook and restore her energy. When she returned to work, she had a new attitude and perspective, and she's never looked back. She's also never forgotten the empathy her boss—who clearly saw that she was in need of a substantial break, not a cosmetic one—showed her.

I like the term "management by empathy," because it's a reminder to keep in mind the feelings and needs of your team, not just the needs of your projects. This is especially important to keep in mind if you, like me, are quite self-sufficient at the office. Since I've never required much "care and feeding" at work, I sometimes forget that everyone else isn't the same way. I was reminded of this in a funny exchange with former Hearst human resources director Ruth Diem as our new building was being completed. On nearly every floor except the corporate one, the offices had glass walls, with no blinds, shades, or curtains. This made for a very open environment, which was exactly what we were looking for, but it didn't offer anything in the way of privacy.

At one point Ruth said to me, "Cathie, we need to make sure there's a place where people can have a little privacy—where people can go to cry."

"We do?" I asked, surprised. "How many people cry at work?"

"Plenty," she laughed. But her point was valid, and it's something that wouldn't have occurred to me. She was taking into consideration the needs of our employees, even if they might have been different from her own. It's not a skill that comes naturally to everyone, but it's certainly one worth cultivating. (By the way, we did actually create an enclosed space where people could go for a rest, or a private moment to collect themselves.)

As I've learned over the years, there is one foolproof way to make sure you know and understand your employees' needs and concerns. And though it sounds simple, it actually requires more work to pull off than you'd think:

Be the best listener you can be.

If there's one skill that I've worked hard to learn, this is it. It's arguably the most important skill you need as a leader, because it affects every element of your team's productivity.

It's easy to hear what you want to hear from people, and much more difficult to actually take in their meanings and motivations. But once you start listening—*really* listening—you'll be surprised at how much you'll learn. And not only that, the very fact that you are listening will encourage others to express themselves. While you're at it, remember that listening involves more than just hearing a person's words. It's also taking in tone and body language, which are clear cues to how someone is feeling, even if he or she is having trouble expressing it. As the great Yogi Berra once said, "You can observe a lot by watching."

Earlier in my career, I heard a management expert speak on the subject of meetings. "People come to a meeting for one of three different reasons," she said. "One, because they're supposed to. Two, because it's a vacation from whatever else they're doing that day. Or, three, because they're a prisoner." That summary has stuck in my head all these years, because it really brought home the fact that even if we're all in the same room, meeting, or event, other people may be having very different experiences than I am. There are as many dynamics in a room as there are people—and often even more.

This management consultant went on to describe the different ways people communicate in meetings. "Some people want to speak up all the time, and others never want to say a word. This doesn't mean they have nothing to say—it just means they might prefer one-on-one conversations to group ones." As an extrovert, I realized I'd often made unfair assumptions about people's knowledge or skills, based in part on how they performed in group settings. I'd judged them according to how I'd judge myself if I were acting the same way, never considering that we simply had different ways of doing things.

Once I came to that realization, it changed the way I assessed people. It also led me to change my leadership style. Previously, I'd have gone into a meeting and directed it from the start, calling on people to answer certain questions and guiding the conversation. I assumed that leading the conversation was the best way to be a leader. Now I usually open meetings with just a short summary of why we're there, and what we hope to accomplish. Then I sit back and listen as others take over. It's amazing how much I've learned that I might otherwise have missed.

Yes, sometimes leadership involves knowing when not to lead. That's because

> **Great leaders are great delegators.**

Learning to delegate is one of the hardest skills to develop as you move up the corporate ladder, yet it's also one of the most crucial. You can't become an effective leader by doing everything yourself, partly because the higher you go, the more tasks fall under your purview. If you try to do it all on your own, you'll not only drive yourself crazy, you're certain to fail. Getting buried in minutiae is one of the most common, and most deadly, mistakes you can make while rising up the career ladder. When you're too bogged down in every detail, it's easy to lose sight of the big picture.

Ask yourself this question: "Is there a legitimate reason that this task needs my personal attention?" More often than not, you'll find that the answer is no.

Allowing others to take the lead—in meetings, on projects, or in any aspect of work—accomplishes something deeper, too. It makes other people feel more invested in the outcome, and gives them a sense of accomplishment and ownership that they otherwise wouldn't have; it allows them to shine. There's no better way to keep your team focused, engaged, and fulfilled than by giving them the ability to achieve important goals themselves.

Another quality of good leadership is being able to keep a broader perspective when others might be overly focused on details. It's knowing how to

> **Focus on solutions, not problems.**

In the Prologue, I described Joe Welty's reaction on the day I was introduced as *USA Today*'s new president, when he told me, "I just want you to know up front that I'm not going to be reporting to you." Right from the very start, it was clear that Welty's attitude was going to be a problem.

And, boy, was it ever. For the first couple of months at *USA Today*, Welty tried to draw me into a petty game of one-upmanship. He'd call meetings and deliberately not tell me about them. And whenever I called a meeting to which he was wasn't invited, he'd show up and stand in the doorway, arms folded, as if demonstrating to those assembled that he was still in charge. The growing tension between us trickled down throughout the office. It was becoming a progressively more difficult situation.

I could have gone to Al Neuharth and complained or asked him to find a way to fix it. But that would have violated this important rule: Don't take problems to your supervisor; take solutions. I decided that it would be better to figure out the solution myself and then present it to Neuharth.

Ray Gaulke, my Gannett colleague, helped me come up with a plan. Instead of keeping Welty at *USA Today*, where he would continue to clash with me, why not move him to a comparable position at Gannett? That way, Welty would have equivalent duties, but we wouldn't have to deal with each other directly, and peace would be restored to the office at *USA Today*. It was a simple, straightforward solution that would leave all parties happy. Also, Welty and Neuharth would both save face—always a good goal to strive for.

Ray and I asked Neuharth and *USA Today* publisher Jack Heselden out for dinner to present our plan. We laid it out carefully, point by point. "This will work for everyone involved," I told them. "And we should put it into effect immediately."

Across the table, Neuharth looked unimpressed. He raised a couple of objections, poking and prodding around the edges of our plan. Was I sure Welty's leaving wouldn't negatively impact our advertising progress at *USA Today*? The financial situation was tough at *USA Today*, after all, so every ad sale was critical. Had I covered all the bases in terms of who would pick up the slack when Welty left? Was this really the best plan for the newspaper—or was it just my way of getting rid of someone I was clashing with?

Ray and I answered Neuharth's questions one after the other, hoping we were making headway. Then, suddenly, Neuharth leaned forward with a smirk, reached into his jacket pocket, and pulled out a piece of paper. With a theatrical flourish, he un-folded it and started to read. It was a draft press release, obviously prepared before the dinner, announcing the very move that we had been pushing for: Joe Welty was to be named executive vice-president of Gannett Media Sales, the newly created division that Ray Gaulke was heading.

Ray and I were dumbfounded. I had to laugh—for all my worrying about whether Neuharth would go for the plan, he obviously was a step ahead of us. It was one of the many times that, despite his quirks and provocations, I had to marvel at Neu-harth's uncanny ability to anticipate and see around a corner. It was one of his best qualities as a leader.

I liked Al Neuharth, and we enjoyed a good working rela-tionship. He could be loose and funny, and he even took it well when I occasionally teased him about something. That said, you always knew who was boss at *USA Today*. He never allowed that line to blur, which is the next key leadership quality on our list:

> **Learn the difference between playing and coaching.**

When I first met Michael Clinton, he had just left Condé Nast after thirteen years, and had been recommended as some-one I should hire if I could get him. Michael is an incredibly

well-rounded person—not only a very good publishing executive, but a world traveler, accomplished photographer, pilot, and
excellent public speaker. I'd heard all this about Michael and
knew he'd be impressive when I met him. But what I didn't realize was how much I'd like him personally. Condé Nast's loss
would be Hearst's gain.

From our first meeting, over drinks at Mickey Mantle's restaurant on Central Park South in Manhattan, Michael and I got
along as though we'd known each other forever. We talked for
several hours, surprised to find how naturally our conversation
flowed and how much our ideas were in sync. Michael and I
wrote out contract terms on a napkin at that first meeting, and
he started work at Hearst very soon after that.

Because Michael reports to me, our relationship is different
from what it would be if we worked in different companies; even
though we're very friendly, it's always clear that we're colleagues
first, and pals second. The reality is, most people don't want
their boss to act like their best friend, and a boss who aspires to
friendship with employees is blurring the line in an unhealthy
way. After all, you're the one who has to make hard decisions on
hiring, firing, and other tricky personnel moves, so you don't
want to complicate those decisions unnecessarily.

You might not think that the friend-employer dynamic is
such a big issue in the workplace. But in a recent survey quoted
in *USA Today,* when more than nine hundred workers were
asked, "What is your boss's greatest sin?" the number-one answer
was "Being everyone's friend." It's a big problem, not only because
it complicates working relationships, but also because it can lead
to resentment among employees, who may see favoritism even
when there is none. So make it easy on yourself and others, and
keep those lines intact.

• • •

IN late 1995, shortly before I came to Hearst, CEO Frank Bennack had decided to make an editorial transition at *Cosmopolitan*. Helen Gurley Brown had been editor-in-chief at *Cosmo* for three decades—an extraordinary run in the magazine business, and a testament to her dedication, skill, and loyalty to the company. At the time, Helen was in her seventies, and with a new editor scheduled to come in, what could Hearst offer her now? She still came to the office every day, arriving early and staying late, and she was as devoted to *Cosmo* as ever.

After thought and discussion among Hearst's top magazine execs, a new position was created just for Helen: editor-in-chief of *Cosmopolitan*'s international editions. It was perfect. *Cosmo* has an unprecedented worldwide presence, and offering Helen a role in expanding and improving the international editions was the best possible outcome for everyone. It allowed her to continue to be involved in the magazine, and it meant that Hearst would continue to benefit from her presence and input.

The choice to create a position for Helen points up one of the qualities I love most about the Hearst Corporation: the company-wide practice of treating employees and former employees with loyalty and respect. It's a generous, admirable inclination, which leads us to our next lesson in being a good leader:

> **Loyalty isn't just for dogs.**

When I first started at Hearst, I thought it was odd that several of the offices on the corporate floor were often empty, yet assistants toiled dutifully outside them. Eventually I realized that these were the offices of people who had retired after working decades for Hearst. Thanks in large part to Frank Bennack, for whom loyalty is a hard-and-fast credo, most retiring top executives were given the option of keeping an office, so they could remain part of the corporate life even in retirement.

Hearst's loyalty to its employees is well known in the industry, so I was all the more surprised when Bonnie Fuller challenged it in a very significant way. There are many things I admire about Bonnie, but this was a time when her ambition caused her to overstep.

In 1992, Hearst hired a dynamic, accomplished British magazine editor named Liz Tilberis to run *Harper's Bazaar,* one of our oldest and most prestigious titles. Liz and her family moved to New York, and she quickly became a darling in the fashion world, with her charm, wit, and down-to-earth approach to her life and work. Then, about a year into her job, she was diagnosed with ovarian cancer—one of the most difficult types of cancer to beat. Her prognosis was not good.

Liz fought the disease bravely, and continued to work every day she was well enough to do so. Over the course of six years, she had good weeks and bad weeks, but she never shirked her duties at *Harper's Bazaar.* Her struggle was well known throughout the magazine and fashion worlds, and in an industry that prizes physical appearance, she left any pretense of vanity by the wayside. She kept her hair in a pixie cut and continued to come to work during and after chemotherapy. Liz was determined not to let cancer beat her, and to edit the magazine through whatever came.

Meanwhile, Bonnie, who had been editor-in-chief of *Cosmo* for a couple of years, openly made it known that she'd like to become the next editor of *Harper's Bazaar.* Unfortunately, she did so while Liz was still soldiering on as editor but clearly losing her battle. Frank Bennack had made a commitment to Liz that she would be the editor of *Harper's* as long as she lived—a characteristically loyal position for Frank (and Hearst) to take. There was no way we would replace Liz, not when she was fighting so very hard to do the job we'd hired her to do.

At one point in the spring of 1998, while Liz was particularly sick, Bonnie told Frank she wanted a guarantee in writing that she would become *Harper's Bazaar* editor upon Liz's death. Frank, not surprisingly, said no. His sense of propriety would never allow him to make such a deal with Bonnie—not while Liz was alive.

Bonnie, meanwhile, had gotten an offer from Condé Nast, and it was clear that she'd take it if we didn't promise her the *Harper's Bazaar* job. She was impatient and insistent, but Hearst simply was not willing to guarantee what she wanted. So Bonnie left Hearst, accepting Condé Nast's offer to become the editor of *Glamour.*

We lost a talented magazine editor. Yet by showing loyalty to Liz Tilberis, who died in the spring of 1999 having worked at *Harper's Bazaar* right up to the end, we did the right thing. It's a decision no one here at Hearst has ever regretted. Which leads us right into our next behind-the-scenes quality of great leadership:

> **The ethical decision is always the right decision.**

Over the last five years, there seems to have been an explosion in white-collar crime. Corporate scandals, CEOs throwing lavish personal parties with company money, stock option backdating—bad corporate behavior has been rising, and television images of handcuffed executives being led to prison have become an increasingly common sight.

Obviously, you don't want to break the law in the course of doing your job. But acting ethically at work goes beyond that. It's making decisions based on something more than just making money, expanding a product, or advancing your career. While it's tempting to cut corners and push boundaries, it really is possible to succeed while keeping your ethics 100 percent intact. For example, in the early years of *Ms.* magazine, before the anti-smoking movement had really taken hold, we had a big advertising schedule from Philip Morris, the tobacco company. Philip Morris was a huge advertiser in magazines, and we'd been running their Marlboro ads for some time. Then the company began a new campaign, for a brand called Virginia Slims.

Virginia Slims was a cigarette aimed specifically at female smokers, so it was natural that Philip Morris would want to run ads in women's magazines, including *Ms.* The campaign, which featured photos of stylishly dressed women in designer outfits, had a memorable slogan—"You've come a long way, baby"—which quickly became a well-known catchphrase. Virginia Slims also sponsored high-profile tennis tournaments, and produced an annual calendar with quotes and stories about famous women.

I'd met with the Virginia Slims brand manager, Ellen Merlo, and she was ready to make a commitment to buy ads in *Ms.* We got the prototype ads from her, and I took them back to the office to show editor Gloria Steinem, who kept a close eye on anything and everything that went into *Ms.* Because we were a feminist publication, with a specific mission to advance the cause of women, Gloria was always vigilant about what ads, stories, and photographs appeared in the magazine.

I took the ad into Gloria's office, and she looked it over. After a moment she said, "I'm sorry. We can't run this."

"Why not?" I asked. "What's wrong with it?"

"For one thing," Gloria said, "it gives the impression that smoking is a sign of progress. To say, 'You've come a long way, baby,' with the image of a woman smoking, is giving entirely the wrong message. And for another thing," she went on, "the word 'baby' is infantilizing to women." She felt strongly that the ad campaign was condescending.

As the advertising manager, I hated to see us refuse any ads, and frankly, *Ms.* was in no financial position to turn down revenue. Gloria agreed to a compromise: we would run a small ad for the Virginia Slims calendar and see how the readers responded to it.

Gloria's instincts had been right on. When the small Virginia Slims calendar ad ran, the magazine received dozens of letters of protest from readers, despite the fact that it advertised the calendar, not the cigarettes themselves. The readers of *Ms.* had a very proprietary feeling about "their" magazine, and this had clearly pushed their buttons.

Gloria could still have chosen to run the ads despite the feedback, but she held firm. This wasn't what *Ms.* was about, and although we needed the revenue the ads would have brought, she felt strongly that accepting them would compromise our mission and our ethics. From a business perspective, I didn't much care for her decision. But from an ethical perspective, and in terms of living up to the mission and goals of *Ms.*, I completely understood why she made it.

Unfortunately, the decision to turn down Virginia Slims resulted in Philip Morris pulling all their ads from *Ms.*, a move that cost us $250,000 in the first year of the boycott alone. This was a huge financial blow, and it only got worse. Philip Morris refused to advertise in *Ms.* for the next sixteen years, costing the magazine untold millions of dollars.

No one ever said it was easy to follow the ethical path. But I know Gloria Steinem never regretted her choice, nor should she have. *Ms.* survived the boycott with its mission, its conscience, and its readers intact, and in the long run, that's what matters most. Making ethical choices is generally a good business decision, too, since consumers tend to feel more loyal to companies they feel personally good about.

This story also points up another key lesson in leadership.

Gloria Steinem never shrank from taking responsibility for her decision, no matter how much money it cost the magazine. She had the ability as a true leader to

---

Remember where the buck stops.

One of the most difficult parts of my job comes when we have to close down a magazine. There's nothing harder than facing a room full of people who've given their all to make a magazine work, and telling them we're pulling the plug. All the same, I always make a point of delivering the news myself. I could send another high-ranking Hearst executive to do it, but as the president of Hearst Magazines, I've always felt keenly that the buck stops with me. If I'm willing to take credit for our successes, I have to be equally prepared to take blame for losses. Anything less would be a dodge.

The same is true for any successes and failures in the office. Have you ever had a boss who

- shifted blame for failures onto his team, even if they resulted from his own poor leadership?

- sought out scapegoats in an ongoing effort to make herself look good to her own boss?

- forced subordinates to take on unpleasant tasks that he should have done himself?

All these tendencies are far too common in the workplace, and they're devastating to team cohesiveness and performance. As a boss, you might think you're showing leadership skills by portraying yourself as an error-free example, but your team knows better. And knowing that their boss is dodging responsibility provokes only bitterness and disaffection.

It sounds strange to say it, but a big component of being an effective leader is simply choosing to lead and taking responsibility for what comes. Another poll quoted in *USA Today* revealed that in a survey of nearly a thousand people, fully 71 percent said they did *not* want to be the boss. Only 26 percent said they'd like to be the boss, with the rest undecided, which tells you something about how fearful or unwilling people are to step up and take responsibility.

There's one other saying about leadership: It's easy to be a good-time leader, but it's the bad times that separate the leaders from the managers. So don't be afraid to step up in the bad times and take responsibility. Your team, and your bosses, will appreciate it more than you know.

Similarly, when something goes wrong and you've had a hand in it—whether you're the leader or farther down the totem pole—don't be afraid to step up and take responsibility. Denying responsibility won't make you look better or exonerate you; in fact, it will have the opposite effect. Confess swiftly, apologize, and propose a solution for moving forward. Everyone on your team will appreciate you more for it.

EARLY in my career, at a time when diversity in the corporate suite meant middle-aged white men who belonged to different country clubs, Al Neuharth made the radical move of appointing women as publishers of several Gannett newspapers. One was Sue Clark-Johnson, whom he promoted to publisher of the *Niagara Gazette.*

"Sue," Neuharth told her, "the publisher is retiring. Are you interested in the position?"

"Do you think I'm ready?" she asked him.

"Of course not," he told her, "but I've never been ready for any job I've done. If you do a bad job, I'll just fire you. If you do a good job I'll promote you." And that was that. Sue ended up doing a terrific job, and continued moving up the corporate ladder within Gannett, where today she is the president of the newspaper division.

I love this story, because it sums up perfectly Al Neuharth's attitude toward diversity in the workplace. He honestly didn't care where people went to school, what color their skin was, or whether they were men or women. All he cared about were results, and he made that clear time and again, not just verbally but in the hires he made. Life at Gannett was a real meritocracy, years before that idea came into vogue in the business world. (As we used to joke, Gannett was one of the few companies where, at management meetings, there was a line outside the ladies' room.) It's an excellent reminder of our next rule of good leadership:

Throw everyone into the pool.

Earlier in this chapter, I wrote that good leaders give their teams the chance to achieve important goals on their own. Neuharth simplified this point even further. In his words, he'd "throw people into the pool to see if they could swim." He gave people the opportunity to succeed, and if they took advantage of it, all the better for them—and, of course, for Gannett.

For Neuharth, diversity was a goal. You could argue that he pursued it because it was the right thing to do, but that wasn't why he did it. He did it because it made smart business sense. For one thing, you can't reach diverse audiences if you're not a diverse company. Any company that has a monolithic team of same-gender, same-ethnicity employees will understand how to market products to their particular group, but in today's changing society, that's a recipe for only marginal success, if not outright failure. Over the last couple of decades the face of America has changed, not just in terms of how we look and where we're from, but how we choose to identify ourselves.

When I was growing up in Chicago, it was a very ethnically divided city. When you first met someone, they were likely to ask you, "What are you?" And in my case, the answer was "Irish," because people tended to identify themselves according to their ethnic background. Now, of course, that question seems outdated, partly because increasing numbers of Americans come from mixed-race homes, and partly because we just don't think in those terms so much anymore. As American society becomes increasingly multicultural, companies need to shift their thinking on how they market to consumers—or face the consequences.

It also helps to remember that hiring people with different backgrounds, ages, temperaments, and experience pays off big in terms of how your team functions. It's best to mix it up, as hiring people like yourself simply brings you more of the same perspective and skills, rather than the diversity of skills that more often leads to success. So don't be afraid to throw everyone into the pool. You might be surprised at who your best swimmers turn out to be.

Assembling a great team is the first step in great leadership. Once you've got that team on board, the second step is to help them work as efficiently as possible. One way to do that is to:

Learn to compartmentalize.

Do you ever

- find your mind wandering while in meetings as you think about all the other work you need to do?

- get stuck on a particular task because you can't focus on a new one unless the first is completely finished?

- get distracted by trying to do too much at once and end up doing everything halfway, but nothing well?

- have trouble leaving your work stress at the office? Or allow stress at home to cast a cloud over your work?

These are common problems, and they're all the result of an inability to compartmentalize. That sounds a bit clinical, so let me explain what I mean.

At its most basic, to *compartmentalize* means to focus on one thing at a time. It's an important skill for anyone to have, especially anyone who aspires to a leadership post. The tone of any department, organization, or business is set at the top, and employees will respond in kind to how their executives lead. An executive who is scattered and distracted will find that her team responds in kind, so it pays to work on this skill.

How can you do that? Well, if you're in a meeting, don't sit there constantly checking your BlackBerry. Believe me, whatever it is can wait—and if it really can't, you probably shouldn't be in the meeting to begin with. When you're on the phone with someone, focus on what they're saying, not on responding to email or tidying up your desk. You might think that you save time by focusing on multiple tasks, but you'll probably just end up needing to ask the person on the other end of the line to repeat things, which just wastes more time.

Focus fully and listen fully, and when you leave the office at

the end of the day, leave your work stress there. Just about everyone is better off taking time away from the job, because it serves
to refresh and renew one's perspective. Even if you're the boss,
that doesn't mean you have to live at the office or never think
about anything else. In my experience, the best bosses—and the
happiest people—are those who have something to go home to
after they've locked the office door behind them.

It's also important to

Know when to step back.

One afternoon I got a call from Ellen Levine, who was then
the editor-in-chief of *Good Housekeeping*. She'd just had a heated
argument with another editor, and was calling to fill me in on the
situation. "We had an eruption," Ellen said—a statement that
concerned me, since she was a relatively unflappable person.

What should I do? I thought about it the rest of the day,
and decided that rather than inserting myself in the middle, I'd
stay on the sidelines and see if they could sort it out themselves.
This wasn't easy to do; I wanted this dispute resolved before it
had a chance to turn into a real feud. It was a gamble, but I chose
to trust in their ability to work it out.

Three days went by, and then finally, on the fourth day,
Ellen called to say they had resolved the situation themselves. I
was hugely relieved. I'd been worried when I didn't hear back,
but in the end, the fact that Ellen and the editor had resolved the
issue on their own, rather than having a solution imposed from
above, boded well for their relationship moving forward.

It's never easy to let go, even when the crisis seems small or
temporary. But often these are the best times to do so, since they

allow your team to exercise their own abilities to solve problems. And stepping back is one more proof that

> **There's more than one way to succeed.**

In interviews, I'm often asked what lessons I've learned from other business leaders. Through serving on two corporate boards, those of Coca-Cola and IBM, I've been fortunate enough to meet and observe several high-profile, very successful CEOs. I've read their books, seen them give speeches, been their dinner partners, and read interviews they've given. Interestingly, the most important lesson I've taken from my contact with these men and women is that there is no single set of rules for how to succeed, and that trying to copy what someone else has done won't help.

I've enjoyed a lot of personal success in my career, and the companies and organizations I've worked for have done well, too. But everything that has worked for me—my personal leadership style, career choices, and skill set—makes up only one recipe for success. At its most basic level, success is born out of recognizing and using your unique skills, working hard and working smart, and following your gut instincts. Never let any so-called guru make you think that there's a one-size-fits-all prescription. There isn't.

If there is one quality that all the CEOs I know share, it is that they're all remarkably comfortable in their own skin. So trust yourself, and listen to your natural instincts. It's the best way to figure out your own personal path to success.

* * *

WHILE I was at *Ms.* magazine, a friend of Pat Carbine's named Ronnie Eldridge was running for the New York City Council. Pat encouraged us to get involved in her campaign, so we held a couple of wine-and-cheese fund-raisers, with bottles of cheap red wine and big platters of cheese cubes. They were modest affairs, and invariably brought in very small sums of money— maybe a couple hundred dollars for two hours' worth of work. It occurred to me that women had yet to realize that if you want to put someone in office, you have to write checks to help make it happen.

So I got the name of a professional fund-raiser and called to ask her advice. We met for breakfast, and I told her about our efforts up to then to raise money for Ronnie. What she told me in response has stuck with me all these years.

"Honey," she said, "you don't know the first thing about fund-raising. Here's the most important thing. When you want to raise money for someone, you need to do it in someone's home. You need them to stand up in front of the crowd and say, 'I personally will contribute five hundred dollars,' or however much. Because everyone who accepts an invitation to a fund-raiser wants to know how little they can get away with giving once they're there. So once the hostess puts a number on it— that's what they'll give."

It was as though a lightbulb had been switched on. The advice made perfect sense, and it made me want to go back out there and raise some real money for Ronnie, and for other candidates and causes that I cared about. Which brings us to the next key element of being a great leader:

> **Practice generosity.**

Leadership on the personal level is every bit as important as leadership on the business level. There are numerous ways to use your talents and time for good causes. You can volunteer, serve on nonprofit boards, give money, arrange fund-raisers. All of these are critical ways to display leadership. And they also have ancillary benefits for you.

Volunteering and/or serving on nonprofit boards, for example, is an excellent way to give back to the community while expanding your circle of connections. Charitable organizations, museums, colleges and universities, nonprofit radio and television stations, opera and ballet companies, community theaters—all these organizations need time, money, and energy to stay afloat. When you give, you enrich not just the recipient, but yourself.

In addition, it's a great way to keep yourself attuned to issues you might not ordinarily have thought about. I'm on the board of trustees of the University of Notre Dame, and at first I found it difficult at our three-times-a-year meetings not to focus on what I needed to be doing right then back at Hearst. But then, as I got increasingly engaged in discussions about this great university, I felt mentally stimulated and alert in a completely different way from my life at Hearst. I found it invigorating.

Volunteering your services, time, and money is a great way to achieve satisfaction that your job might not necessarily provide. And your example in this area will trickle down to others in your department or organization. Just make sure that whatever you're doing is allowed by your employer or the government—as I forgot to do one memorable time while at *USA Today*.

I had decided to host a political fund-raiser for my dear friend and mentor, George Hirsch, who was running for Congress. I wanted to hold it at Gannett's corporate suite at the Waldorf Towers, one of the most prestigious addresses in New York. With its lavish interiors, including marble-floored lobbies and beautiful chandeliers, the Waldorf Towers has housed numerous famous residents over the years, including Frank Sinatra, Cole Porter, Mamie Eisenhower, and the Duke of Windsor. The Gannett suite was quite an impressive place—perfect for hosting a fund-raiser—so I made plans through Al Neuharth's assistant to reserve it.

After the invitations went out, I got a call from the publisher of the New York *Daily News,* whom I had invited. "Wow," he said, "I'm really surprised you can do this."

"Do what?" I asked.

"Host a political fund-raiser as publisher of *USA Today,*" he replied. "You represent a newspaper—normally that's considered a conflict of interest."

Whoops, I thought. *Here we go.*

USA Today was my first job at a newspaper, as opposed to magazines, where hosting a political fund-raiser might not be considered a conflict. I knew I'd blundered, and so I called Neuharth right away to let him know what was going on.

Neuharth was livid. "You're doing *what?*" he barked. "Cathie, how could you not realize this was inappropriate? This might be a local election and wouldn't get covered editorially by *USA Today,* but still, it doesn't send the right message."

"I'm sorry, Al," I said. "I can cancel it, but the invitations are out."

Neuharth thought for a moment, then said with annoyance, "Just don't do it again."

Fortunately, I got out of that one without a scratch, but I was much more careful about my political activities from that point on. And no matter how much time and energy my philanthropic and political activities have taken over the years—and they definitely do require work—I've always been glad to pursue them. Showing generosity and civic awareness is a great way to repay the legacies of those who've opened doors for you and to help others. So give back: it's the right thing to do, in business and in life. And it might even get you recognized at work in a way you wouldn't have been otherwise, making it a smart business decision, too.

BLACK & WHITE

Advice from All Over

Many friends and colleagues helped with this book by recalling stories and anecdotes from over the years. Here are some of the best—a compendium of things I wish I'd known when I was just starting out.

MISTAKES

You can make a big mistake, and you can make a bad mistake. Just don't make a big, bad mistake.

I first heard this saying from my former boss at Hearst, Frank Bennack. Frank is one of the most even-keeled executives I've ever known, with a yarn or quip for every situation, but even so, I feel very fortunate that I never made a big, bad mistake under his watch. I'm not sure exactly what would have happened, but I wouldn't have wanted to see it, much less be the cause of it.

Don't panic. Ever.

This is an excellent piece of advice—especially if you've just made a big, bad mistake. Panicking is a natural reaction, but it's also the quickest way to compound whatever trouble you've suddenly found yourself in. If you stay calm, you'll restore calm. And remember, panicking has never fixed anything. It only prolongs and intensifies the agony.

Remember, too, that your body language says as much as your words. People are always observing the look on the boss's face or the way you carry yourself. In our new Hearst Tower, we have a long escalator that runs between the lobby and the third floor. Everyone can see you, which is why, no matter how long, tiring, or bad my day might have been, I make a point of looking friendly and pleasant on the ride up and down. No one wants to see the boss with a sour look on her face.

Thinking you have something all figured out is usually the first sign that you don't.

There are often more sides to an issue than you think, and situations can change at the drop of a hat, so be careful when assuming you've got everything completely figured out.

CRISES

A crisis for you may not be one for your boss.

One day, one of our editors called me about a situation that was brewing. Her message said it was a crisis, but because I knew what the problem was, and knew it wasn't critical, I hadn't yet called her back. I told my husband, Tom, about her latest voice mail—"Cathie, this is a crisis!"—and Tom said, "Well, here's another way to think of it. It may be a crisis for her, but it's not a crisis for you." With that observation, Tom crystallized the issue.

Remember that what feels like a crisis for you is not necessarily one for your boss. And act accordingly.

Never take a supporting role in somebody else's drama.
It's always tempting to be sucked into the whirlwind of office drama, but it rarely produces anything but a headache. When you see a melodrama developing, that's the best time to go out and have a long lunch.

Even a monkey sometimes falls from a tree.
I love this saying because it's so true, and so easy to forget. Monkeys might be the best climbers in the animal kingdom, but even though they have a natural talent and are uniquely built for it, even *they* sometimes fall from trees. It's a valuable lesson to remember whenever you fail at something you're good at. Just climb right back up that tree.

RESPONSIBILITY

A good team member takes more than her share of the blame and less than her share of the credit.
Don't go overboard with this one; as discussed in an earlier chapter, you shouldn't simply hand over all the credit if some or all is rightfully yours. But being a good team member means stepping up for your teammates, and this is an excellent way to do just that.

It's okay to ignore the first big mistake and forgive the second. But the third? Then we've got problems.
When dealing with others, it's fine to give people a little leeway. But once they've demonstrated a propensity for screwing up, it's your job to call them on it and get the situation fixed.

CREATIVITY AND VISION

Give people a road map.
In a speech, presentation, or directive, keep in mind one simple rule of thumb: Tell people what you're going to say, say it, and then tell them what you just said. There's no better way to ensure that you get your point across.

In the contest between style and substance, substance always wins. The only variable is timing.
Style, like hype, is not a bad thing. But it's only valuable if it is accompanied by substance. Otherwise it's little more than vapor that will be wafted away by the first breeze.

Create a vision. People like to know where they are headed, and they'll get on board if they know where you want them to go. Establishing a clear vision is the way to inspire a team, create a product, and start down the path to success. Everything flows from that.

COMMUNICATION

To make something clear to others, you first have to make it clear to yourself.
I love this advice, because it's so obvious and yet so commonly ignored. Half the battle of good communication has nothing at all to do with communicating to others—it's figuring things out fully in your own head first.

It's okay to let people see you're angry, but it's not okay to lose your cool.
There's a big difference between these two emotions: losing your cool is an overly personalized response in an office environment.

It's better to express anger briefly, then move quickly to the next, much more important step: fixing whatever's been broken.

TALENT

When you look at talent, look for a track record of success, not just the most recent success.
It's easy to get caught up in someone's latest, greatest achievements, but business, as well as life, is a marathon, not a sprint. A person who has shown an ability to achieve over the long haul will invariably prove far more valuable than the latest, greatest flash in the pan.

As Mark Twain wrote, "Noise proves nothing. Often a hen who has merely laid an egg cackles as if she has laid an asteroid."
Every workplace has its share of cacklers, but when all is said and done, it's production rather than self-promotion that counts.

Everyone must row with the oars he [or she] has.
As this old English proverb has it, there will always be things you're naturally good at, and things you're not. The sooner you learn to focus on the former rather than the latter, the better off you'll be—in every part of your life.

GOALS

In a new job, once you have the lay of the land, set three big goals that you'd like to accomplish in the first year.
If you get two accomplished, they'll be noticed and you'll be seen as a contributor. It's far easier to achieve goals once you've taken the time to identify them, yet setting ambitious yet achievable goals remains one of the most underappreciated skills. Take a

step back from the day-to-day busywork that threatens to swallow us all, and assess the broader picture. Picture your goals, write them down, and then work to fulfill them. That's the essence of productivity.

Don't let yourself have an itch you can't scratch.
This sounds simple, but for some people it's an incredibly difficult piece of advice to follow. We've all encountered people who always seem to want what they can't have and who obsess over things they can't change. There's nothing wrong with high aspirations, but if you're setting unfulfillable goals for yourself, you'll just end up frustrated.

A no is never a no—it just means you haven't given them enough information.
This is a famous old saying in sales; what it really means is, don't give up the first time you hear the word *no*. Very often, people can be—and even want to be—convinced. Don't miss an opportunity to get the *yes* you want because you weren't persistent enough.

TIME

Don't let the urgent steal from the important.
Has this ever happened to you? You have to write a big report that's due by the end of the day, but the phone never stops ringing, the email messages keep coming, colleagues keep popping in and asking for help—and by 6:00 p.m., you've done everything *except* the one task you really truly needed to finish. Letting the urgent steal from the important means getting distracted by the secondary tasks that pile up on your desk each day. Just be-

cause something has an immediate deadline doesn't mean it's the most important thing on your desk. Make a list of what you need to accomplish, rank everything according to importance, and don't stray from it.

If you want something done, give it to a busy person.
I love this phrase because it's so counterintuitive and yet so true. People who have too little to do often end up wasting time, while those with full plates tend to work at full speed until everything's done. Look around at your office mates; chances are, the ones who appear the busiest are also the ones who are most reliable.

Don't look at your emails when you first come into your office.
I'll admit that I don't always have the strength to follow this advice, which comes from management expert Julie Morgenstern. But whenever I do, I'm invariably glad I did. There's a quicksand pit of email that we all slide into at the beginning of each day, and it's easier to stay out of it for the first hour or two and get important things done than to sink into it and then try to pull yourself out and regain your footing.

Only let a piece of paper cross your desk once.
Here's another piece of advice I don't always succeed in following, but it's a great one from advertising legend David Ogilvy, author of *Confessions of an Advertising Man,* who never let any memo, letter, or report cross his desk more than one time. He was relentless about either passing it along to someone else, acting on whatever needed doing, or simply throwing it away. If you're the kind of person who has piles of ancient notes, letters, and memos cluttering your desk, take this advice to heart.

OFFICE POLITICS

Squash office politics before it becomes half your day's work and counterproductive to your company's mission.
Smart leaders and managers act to control office politics before it gets out of hand. Make it clear that in your workplace, office politics is out.

Don't pick a fight unless there is at least a 50 percent chance you can win.
When you lose a fight, you not only fail to achieve the goal you were fighting for, you also lose political capital. So if you know you're going to lose, it's better to stay out of it to begin with, and save your political capital for a fight you're more likely to win.

THE BIG PICTURE

The first half of your life is spent chasing success; the second half is spent chasing significance.
There will come a time in your career, if it hasn't already arrived, when you'll begin to think about the legacy you'll leave behind. And suddenly the scrapping and climbing you've been doing, and the energy you've spent trying to advance, will seem less important than the larger meaning behind your work and your life. If you start thinking in those terms now, you'll accomplish more, with greater satisfaction, than you thought possible. Don't wait until the end of your career to think about the meaning of your work.

CHAPTER 9

The Future Is Now

Not long ago I was with my nineteen-year-old son, Duffy, signing him up for a new cell phone plan. When the sales rep asked, "Do you want insurance, in case you lose the phone?" Duffy immediately said, "No, I don't need that. My phone's always with me."

I thought about this for a moment and realized Duffy was right; his phone is literally always with him, in his pocket, no matter where he is. I've seen him answer it in stores, in the car, in the elevator, even at the dinner table (for which I nearly ripped it out of his hand!). And I realized that for Duffy and most of his generation, the notion of being connected at all times isn't a new or groundbreaking idea. It's simply their reality, and has been for their whole lives.

This might sound like a pretty minor revelation, but it shows how quickly expectations can change. Even ten years ago, only a relative handful of people had cell phones and used them regularly. Cell phones were just beginning to enter the mainstream then, so they weren't the province of teenagers and children. But now practically everyone who's old enough to talk in complete sentences has one. And that's just one small component of the revolution that has taken place over the last decade.

When I first started at Hearst in late 1995, I was surprised to find that most of the company wasn't using email yet. At that time our magazine staffs were spread out among ten to twelve different buildings in Manhattan, but instead of taking advantage of the efficiencies of email, most of our top-tier magazine executives still communicated through telephone calls, faxes, and even messengered letters. It was unbelievable. Soon after I arrived, we introduced company-wide email, to the dismay of some old-school veterans and the relief of many. Now, of course, no one would dream of trying to work without it—even though my fifteen-year-old daughter, Alison, who's constantly sending text messages over her phone, says, "Email is for old people."

The Internet revolution was a once-in-a-lifetime transformation, so we probably won't see its like again soon. But we'll certainly see other significant changes in how we work, play, and live. As I often tell our magazine editors, "Eighteen months from now, everything will be different. We may not be able to predict exactly how, but we know it will be. So be ready."

It really is impossible to predict the future, so it's important to focus on the one thing you can do—and in fact, must do—to succeed: learn to adapt to changes, whatever they may be. Moving forward: this is the one skill that will help determine how successful and contented you are in your work and in your personal life. Here's a story from my own recent work experience to illustrate what I mean.

For my first ten years at Hearst, I had an executive assistant named Pamela Murphy. Pamela was everything you could want in an assistant—smart, reliable, and personable. She seemed to enjoy working at Hearst, but she had a long commute, so after returning from maternity leave following the birth of her first child, she asked if she could have a flextime arrangement, coming into the office four days a week and working one at home.

I was not a fan of this idea, and told her so. But we agreed she could give it a try for six months to see how it went. At the end of that period, Pamela decided she liked flextime and asked if we could continue the arrangement. I had found it difficult to adjust to having her out of the office one day a week, so I told her no, I needed her here all five days.

Within a year of that conversation, Pamela took a job with a company that was closer to her home, which would cut back drastically on her commute and give her more time with her family. I was surprised, dismayed, and even a little hurt. We had worked together for ten very good years—how could she just leave like this? I hired another assistant to replace her, but I missed Pamela's skills and good humor. And for the first time I really had to consider whether my stance against flextime needed to be more, well, flexible.

I decided it did, and a month after Pamela had left, I asked if she'd be willing to return and work under the conditions she'd suggested before. Fortunately for me, she'd found that her new job wasn't all it was cracked up to be, so she did come back. Now she works four days a week at Hearst and one at home. I still don't love the arrangement, but it's worth it to have her back.

This episode illustrated a couple of things for me. First, the nature of the workplace has changed dramatically even in the past decade. Until very recently, any request to work one day a week at home would have been seen as strange, but today, in certain industries, it has become commonplace. Just recently I asked the head of a large industry association about one of their lawyers and was told, "He works three days a week." This would have been unheard of a few years ago, but she didn't even blink when telling me. It's just another working arrangement.

Second, for women in their thirties today, the balance of work versus personal life seems much more important than in past decades. When I was in my thirties, working women felt that they had to push and push and push in order to advance. There was an adage then that we accepted as fact: "As a woman, you have to be twice as good as a man to get half the recognition." If we wanted to succeed then, we didn't have the option of balancing our personal and work lives. But today such a balance is possible, and women like Pamela want to take advantage of it. It's one of the changes that makes me proudest about having been a woman on the front lines during the feminist era.

Third, technology has progressed to a point where it's much easier now for people to work efficiently from home. The differences between Pamela's first and second flextime stints are profound, even though they occurred only a couple of years apart. Now, when someone dials Pamela's number at Hearst, the call is instantly rerouted to her computer at home, and she answers it using a headset; the caller never knows she isn't at her desk there. Pamela's computer software also allows her to see who's calling and transfer calls, just as if she were at Hearst. We've also switched to an electronic scheduler, making it easier to keep track of appointments when she's outside the office. In fact, just about the only thing Pamela can't do when she's at home is peek into the conference room to see when a meeting is breaking up.

Flextime—the arrangement in which an employee spends one or more days out of the office during the week—is just one of many options that have sprung up in the wake of the Internet wave. Some companies have even instituted a "virtual office," where employees don't gather at a central location to work, but work in their homes and communicate electronically, meeting face-to-face only when they've arranged it in advance. In many cases, employees aren't even in the same city or state.

Moving forward, it seems likely these trends will continue. Already a new generation of employees is entering the workforce with the notion that flextime and virtual offices are normal, everyday elements of work life. Casual dress and shorter summer hours are also now common across the board. As an executive, I'm not a fan of all these developments, because there's always a fear that productivity will slip. But as a proponent of the 360° Life, I do like seeing people take steps to balance out their work and personal lives.

So, what other changes might be coming down the pike? I won't presume to claim any special psychic insight, but here are a few trends I would expect to see evolving over time.

THE DIGITAL WORLD

As connectivity becomes faster and more ubiquitous, the Internet will continue to affect businesses—not only in the office, but in the way companies and organizations distribute content. Even three or four years ago, you'd never have read or heard the words *social networking, blogging,* or *YouTube,* and now you can hardly escape them. New technologies will continue to come fast and furious, and the companies that survive and thrive will be those that can adapt to them quickly.

I've always felt that a good motto for adapting to technological change is "Not first, not last." At Hearst, for example, we don't rush to become the first adopters of a new technology, especially since first versions are often flawed and more difficult to use than later versions. But it also doesn't pay to be last, waiting until the rest of the world has leapt ahead.

WIRELESS TECHNOLOGY

After the invention of the Internet, the rise of wireless technology was the second great tech revolution of the late twentieth century. Cell phones, BlackBerrys, Treos, and every other conceivable PDA gadget have changed the way we communicate and work. They're getting smaller and more powerful all the time, and simultaneously liberating us from the workplace and tying us to our work. I love my BlackBerry, because it allows me to get work done during any shred of downtime—in a cab, at the airport, or wherever. On the other hand, it's hard to really, truly take time away from work when it's always right there, at the touch of a button, in your handbag or pocket.

The trick is to learn how to use these technologies without becoming a slave to them. (I confess I haven't always succeeded in this.) If you don't yet have a BlackBerry or Treo, you probably will soon. (Remember, not everyone had a cell phone until recently—now you almost can't find anyone who *doesn't* have one.) Just be sure to set aside some time each day when you're completely "unplugged" and not thinking about work.

NONTRADITIONAL WORK SCHEDULES

As mentioned above, nontraditional work arrangements—from flextime to virtual offices to nontraditional hours—will become even more common. The notion of nine-to-five office hours, with all of us starting our day simultaneously, is fast becoming an anachronism.

Yet as beneficial as it might be for people to work at home or set their own hours, it would be a mistake to lose the many benefits that come from a traditional work environment. When people gather in a common space to work on a common goal, they draw energy from each other, and creativity and innovation are enhanced. There's also more opportunity for serendipitous conversations that lead to great ideas, whereas a person who works at home doesn't have the benefit of face-to-face input that can lead to new ideas.

Even Google, the paradigm for a new, twenty-first-century kind of company, has as its headquarters a gigantic campus where employees are encouraged to spend many hours together beyond the usual nine-to-five. In fact, every possible amenity is offered so that Google employees won't need to leave, from scooters and Segways for getting around internally, to recreation areas where employees can play pool or Ping-Pong, to free snacks and free meals at the Google cafeteria. Even though Google is on the cutting edge with technology, the executives clearly understand that encouraging people to mingle and share ideas is still the best way to spark creativity.

So, even as technology continues to give us new options, it's best not to get overly caught up in the idea of brave new work situations. Sometimes the old way is still the best way.

THE CHANGING SOCIAL CULTURE

As new generations enter the workforce, how will their experiences and expectations affect life at the office? I always try to spend time talking with our interns and entry-level employees at Hearst, and in recent years I've noticed a few trends.

First, there's a culture of expectation that didn't exist before— among young women, certainly (which is a good thing), but also in general. For a generation that grew up watching reality TV shows, the notion that you can win *American Idol*–style success virtually overnight seems deeply ingrained. And today's twenty-somethings also grew up just as the Internet boom demonstrated that anyone, from secretaries on up to company founders, can become a millionaire. There seem to be heightened expectations for good jobs, high salaries, and the kinds of workplace perks we talked about earlier, such as flextime and longer vacations. Younger people also seem to want to be truly fulfilled by their work, rather than simply satisfied.

This may be a by-product of a second trend: this generation is the first in years to come of age during a time of real danger and crisis on our own soil. For young people who were in high school or college during the attacks of September 11, the ensuing six years of elevated security alerts and terrorism scares have had an incalculable impact on their worldview. Understandably, many are focused not simply on getting a good job or making decent money, but also on doing work they find truly fulfilling. Moving forward, as more of these young people graduate from college and take jobs, these trends will continue to influence the workforce.

Finally, as I wrote a few pages ago, this new workforce generation is also superconnected, through sites like MySpace and Facebook, as well as text messaging and cell phones. The idea of what constitutes a "normal" amount of connectedness has changed in society at large, and it will change in the workplace as a result. The generation of employees who relied on handwritten notes and "have your people call my people" is fading away, sooner rather than later. And no matter how you might feel personally about those changes, they're not just inevitable, but here.

AS the examples above show, new trends will continue popping up at the workplace—trends you'll have little or no control over. If that seems frustrating, it just reinforces how important it is to focus on the things you *can* control. You don't need to have psychic ability to predict changes; you just need to be able to realize they're coming and be flexible enough to adapt to them.

IN many ways, the advice above perfectly distills the lessons in this book. After all, if there's one trait that has helped me succeed in my career, it's the ability to learn and change with the times, while continuing to work hard and trust my own instincts. No matter what kind of work you do or what kind of personality you have, this is a skill that's critical to your ultimate success.

That said, remember that although your "ultimate success" is a worthy goal, it's certainly not the only one you should pursue—and it may not even be the most important one. After all, when you leave your workplace at the end of the day, if you then have nowhere else meaningful to go, what will you really have gained with all your hard work? It's far better to be fulfilled in all areas of your life than to sacrifice personal happiness for the sake of advancement. And the good news is you don't *have* to sacrifice it. I'm fortunate enough to be a living testament to that.

As you move toward the future in your career and life, you'll find that the basic lessons of this book—trusting your instincts, adapting to change, pursuing your passion—will be applicable to both your personal life and your career. It really is possible to create a healthy, happy, 360° Life for yourself. I hope the lessons in this book will help you do it.

Epilogue

In the Black

During the time I was writing this book, two meaningful events took place in my life. The first was the official opening of the Hearst Tower, our new company headquarters. For Hearst, this represented a tremendous leap: the construction of the most environmentally "green" skyscraper in New York City, an instant landmark that finally consolidated all our magazine staffs from ten locations in the area, as well as the first major commercial building to have broken ground following the attacks of September 11.

I love the soaring open spaces and state-of-the-art technology of the Hearst Tower. It's a beautiful workspace, and perfect for events; in fact we've already had some amazing evenings here, including the grand opening, when Stevie Wonder played and Mayor Bloomberg, Oprah Winfrey, Katie Couric, and Martha Stewart mingled with hundreds of guests. That night I felt very proud to be a part of this company, and to work in this building. I got so excited, in fact, that I jumped right up on stage with

Stevie Wonder halfway through his set (to the surprise of his band), to dance to a few tunes with our CEO, Vic Ganzi.

Yet the really meaningful moments for me here have been the quiet ones, when I'm alone in my office on the forty-third floor with its views of Manhattan. Sometimes it's the first thing in the morning, when I arrive at work and look out the floor-to-ceiling windows to see an early fog blanketing Central Park, just as the city's lights twinkle awake. The moments I love most, though, are at dusk, when I look out and see the ships cruising up the Hudson River as the sun sets slowly in the distance. These are the times I have to pinch myself, when I think, "Can this really be me, Cathie Black from the South Side of Chicago, here in this beautiful office?"

When I started my career, this all would have seemed like an impossible dream. At that time there really weren't any women presidents of large companies, and there were very few powerful women in politics. For most of the 1970s, there were no women serving in the U.S. Senate, whereas today we have sixteen female senators. We also have the first female Speaker of the House, Nancy Pelosi, and a front-running female candidate for the Democratic presidential nomination in Hillary Clinton.

It's truly a different world, and I'm proud to have been a part of the early group of women executives who helped blaze this trail. As successive generations find less and less resistance in the executive suite, women will one day find themselves on an equal playing field with men. I hope and believe it will come during your career.

The other event in 2006 that really affected me was the death of my mother-in-law, Peg Harvey. She died right after Christmas, at the age of ninety-six, having lived a long, fulfilled life that was characterized by family, friends, and an amazing generosity of spirit.

Peg was raised in Clinton, Iowa, growing up in a modest home during a time of financial uncertainty and upheaval. She lived through the Depression and two world wars, and remembered having gone with her mother to the polls just after women received the right to vote. As a small-town girl in a middle-class family, she could easily have seen the world through the lens of her immediate surroundings. Instead, with a natural curiosity, intelligence, and good humor, she cultivated a view of life much bigger and more far-flung than her roots.

Twenty-five years ago, as I was working my way up the corporate ladder, I married her eldest son, Tom. And when Tom and I adopted our son and daughter, Duffy and Alison, Peg was always there to help out. She always offered unconditional support and love, and even though she'd never worked in business herself—though she might well have if she had been born in a different era—she never once expressed any wish that I'd spend more time with my children and less at the office.

To me, Peg was the embodiment of the 360° Life. She understood how to strike a balance between the different elements of her life, and she never lost focus on finding joy and fulfillment everywhere she could. Her life always extended far beyond the bounds that might have constricted a woman half her age. She loved having friends and family over, and loved telling them about the exploits of her children and grandchildren. She was a natural optimist, a woman who truly embraced life. In fact, before she died, Peg let us know that she didn't want a funeral. She didn't want a big fuss made over her dying, when the fuss, she believed, should be made over living.

My parents died when I was relatively young—my father when I was twenty-two, my mother when I was thirty-five. I was lucky to marry into a family like Tom's, which accepted me as their own from the beginning. Peg always said to me, "What a shame your mother and father weren't around to see your success." I'm fortunate that I had a mother-in-law like Peg to share it with.

I'M not the kind of person who spends a lot of time rehashing things that have already happened. Whether events turn out well or poorly, they're over and done with, and I usually find myself scanning the horizon for the next thing.

Because of that, writing this book has been a fascinating exercise for me, as I've never spent so much time looking back over my career and life. What has struck me time and again, as I've recalled stories and thought of the experiences that have shaped me, is how very lucky I've been. Of course, some people say that you create your own luck, by positioning yourself in the right place and taking advantage of opportunities when they come along, both of which I have always tried to do.

And that's the final piece of advice I'd like to leave you with. Opportunities will come—they always do. Trust yourself enough to jump at them. Never be afraid to go for it. And remember, you deserve to have the best life, and the best career, that you can have.

ACKNOWLEDGMENTS

I mentioned the phrase "It takes a village" earlier in this book, and it's as apt a description of writing a book as any I can imagine. *Basic Black* came to fruition because many people wanted to make it happen and helped make it happen.

First, I'd like to thank my husband, Tom, who's been my help-mate and counsel for more than twenty-five years. He's the most supportive and encouraging partner I could have hoped for, and he's allowed me to spread my wings in ways I might never have imagined.

The greatest blessing we've had was being able to adopt our children, Duffy and Alison. They're young adults now, more fun and interesting than ever to be with. Through the years, they've always kept us young and kept us thinking about the world they're going into. I hope the ideas and messages in this book might be a help to them both.

Three women got me started on this book: Pam Janis, my long-time speechwriter and friend with whom I shared great times at *USA Today*; New York literary agent Frederica Friedman, who first convinced me the time was right to put pen to paper; and our PR guru at

Hearst, my colleague of more than a dozen years, Deb Shriver, who's been urging me for several years to just get it done.

Thanks also to my extraordinary lawyer, Bob Barnett, for his wise advice, and for understanding immediately that this book was for his daughter's generation of recently minted MBAs. It was Bob who led me to Crown senior editor Rachel Klayman—who was, Bob told me from the start, the most insightful editor in the business. We clicked immediately. To the rest of the terrific team at the Crown Publishing Group, especially publishers Jenny Frost, Steve Ross, and Tina Constable, thanks for your enthusiasm and commitment to the project.

Lisa Dickey, my collaborator, was the perfect choice. She sat with me for dozens of hours, attended speeches and meetings, and talked to friends and colleagues, all the while pulling stories and ideas from the far reaches of my mind, some of which were cobwebbed over. But she was always there with a ready laugh or a shake of the head, and she always told me when something didn't make sense or when there wasn't enough of a lesson in the story. She kept an even keel throughout it all and somehow managed to deliver the book on time, despite a move to Los Angeles during final editing.

If I started to thank everyone at Hearst, the list would go on forever. But I owe special thanks to Frank Bennack, of course, who first brought me to Hearst; to Gil Maurer, for his always wise counsel; and to Vic Ganzi, our CEO, who's a great, supportive, understanding, and visionary boss.

Thanks also to Paul Luthringer, Alexandra Carlin, and Nate Christopher, who have helped immeasurably on communications strategy. To Judith Bookbinder, whose eye for design helped to brighten the feel of the book. To Michael Clinton, I sure am glad we signed the napkin that day. We're kindred spirits and have grown a great business—and we're not finished yet. To Valerie Salembier, who's been a part of my life since the *Ms.* days; I'm thrilled for her success at *Harper's Bazaar*. And to Mark Miller, a man of such integrity and brainpower that sometimes it was scary, and who only had Hearst's best interests in mind.

I am so grateful to Kate White, Ellen Levine, and Amy Gross—

these great women of letters. Huge thanks to all of you for holding my hand and for astute editing as the manuscript took shape. You kept saying it was good, and I kept thinking, *Are they only saying that because they work for me?* Special thanks also to Ruth Diem, who assembled a group of younger women at Hearst so we could pick their brains on the life and work balance.

To Oprah Winfrey, thank you for taking that meeting with Ellen and me in January of 1999 and for the gift of allowing us to create your magazine, celebrate its success, and be inspired by you. Thank you for encouraging me to live my best life. Thanks also to Gayle King, without whom the magazine might never have been what it has become.

And then there's Helen Gurley Brown. She's still the first person to dance at our holiday party, in the shortest of skirts and the highest of heels. She's been an icon and an inspiration to women young and old to have a full, exciting, and charged life.

Every successful executive owes a great deal of that success to the people who manage the office. Huge thanks are due to Pamela Murphy, who's now been with me for eleven years, and Tomasina Delaney, who came to Hearst five years ago. They're experts at giving callers and visitors the impression that we're on top of everything and at making them feel they're the only people who matter. For Pamela and Tomasina, no job is too large, no job too small. You always make me look good, and for that, I am deeply appreciative.

Thanks also to the nannies our family has had over the years, particularly Chris Batterton, Michelle McManus, and Colleen Eckert, who have pasted, stapled, and glued our lives together as my career was ascending. You have been a godsend and have helped shaped our children's lives all for the better.

To Gloria Steinem and Pat Carbine, thank you for opening up doors for my generation of women—for encouraging us to dream a big dream and to fulfill our own aspirations. Pat, thank you for convincing all those reluctant, sometimes threatened advertisers that the world was going to be just fine with women leaving their traditional roles.

To Rupert Murdoch, our years together at *New York* were full of great success and a lot of fun. To Joe Armstrong, thanks for being a buddy throughout our magazine careers and thanks most of all for bringing me to *New York* and naming me publisher in an era when that was a first. I know you must have fought hard for it. To George Hirsch, who to this day is a mentor and friend, you were not only a great boss but always gave me sound advice. And before it was encouraged or expected, you gave young women opportunities they wouldn't have gotten at other companies.

Thank you to Al Neuharth, for being the most challenging boss I ever worked for, but also the most inspiring. If it weren't for Al, *USA Today* would never have gotten off the planning blocks. And he's also the guy who opened opportunities for women across the Gannett Company, because he believed in their ability to be great editors and publishers.

To Charles Overby, we had a million laughs and did great business together. To Ray Gaulke, thank God you joined Gannett when I did—I don't think either of us could have toughed it out alone. To George Lois, they threw away the mold when you hit the advertising world. You're a true original.

I hope that the ideas and messages in this book might even be of help to my son as he eventually starts a career. My greatest hope is that he'll dream a big dream and seek a fulfilling life. For my daughter, who may think that the idea of doors being closed to women is all ancient history, I want her to know that we did fight hard so that those who followed could get up the ladder faster and more fairly. Your generation is born to lead. Lastly, since I started by thanking Tom, let me conclude by thanking the family I was born into. My brother, Jim, and sister, Sue, have always been there for me. I have felt buoyed by their pride at every step.

About the Author

CATHLEEN BLACK heads Hearst Magazines, a division of Hearst Corporation and one of the world's largest publishers of monthly magazines. She manages the financial performance and development of some of the industry's best-known titles: *Cosmopolitan; Esquire; Good Housekeeping; Harper's Bazaar; Marie Claire; O, the Oprah Magazine; Popular Mechanics; Redbook;* and *Town & Country*—twenty magazines in all. She also oversees nearly two hundred international editions of those magazines in more than one hundred countries.

Having begun her career in advertising sales with several magazines, including *Holiday* and *Ms.,* she made publishing history in 1979 when she became the first woman publisher of a weekly consumer magazine: *New York.*

Black is widely credited for the success of *USA Today,* where for eight years, starting in 1983, she was first president, then publisher, as well as a board member and executive vice president/marketing of Gannett, its parent company. In 1991 she became president and CEO of the Newspaper Association of America, the industry's largest trade group, where she served for five years before joining Hearst.

She serves as a member of the boards of IBM and the Coca-Cola Company, and held a two-year term as chairman of the Magazine Publishers of America. She is also a board member of the Advertising Council, a trustee of The University of Notre Dame, and a member of the Council on Foreign Relations.

In 2006, Black made *Forbes* magazine's list of "The 100 Most Powerful Women" for the second time, and was listed among *Fortune* magazine's "50 Most Powerful Women in American Business" for the seventh consecutive year. In 2006, she was named "Corporate Publisher of the Year" by the Delaney Report.

Black is a graduate of Trinity College, Washington, D.C., and holds eight honorary degrees.